slow cooker

Fuss-free, slow-cooked family meals

slow cooker

Fuss-free slow cooked family meals

Contents

Hello — 7
How to use your slow cooker — 8
Useful ingredients and equipment — 10
Essential recipe techniques — 12
Adapting the recipes to suit your diet — 14
Foods to avoid for little ones — 17
Storage and freezing guidelines — 18
How to reduce food waste — 20
Keeping kids entertained — 21

Soups & Stews — 22

Pasta — 50

Easy Weeknight — 74

Fakeaway — 102

Weekend Favourites — 122

Conversion chart — 151
Index — 152
Acknowledgments — 159

Hello,

I'm really excited to share with you all of my favourite slow cooker recipes together in one place. I love to use my slow cooker to make my life easier, by quickly prepping the base of the dish in the morning and letting it simmer all day long, filling my house with inviting smells while I look forward to eating later.

Growing up, we always ate around the table together with my mother and siblings. However, it wasn't until I had my daughter, Nina, that I realized why this is so beneficial. Not only does it save you time by cooking just once, it helps to ensure that every member of your family, including you, has the opportunity to sit down and enjoy a good meal together.

It also helps teach our children the physicalities of eating, chewing, and developing cutlery skills, and contributing to forming positive attitudes towards food and nutrition as they grow older.

Offering a wide variety of tastes and textures, while eating together to show your little ones how much you're enjoying the meal, helps children to grow older with reduced tendencies of being fussy with their food. They're watching you, learning from how you eat, and how happy and positive the meal experience is for you – this makes our little ones want to join in and model our behaviours.

If this is the first book of mine you have picked up, let me introduce you to the way I cook. All my recipes are suitable for the whole family from 6 months old, cooking just one meal for the entire family. There is no added salt or excessive sugar within these recipes to make them suitable for little taste testers, and the recipes have been written according to maximize flavour. However, adults do feel free to adjust your plate by adding more seasoning, sweetness, or spice to your portion.

with love from,

How to use your slow cooker

With so many slow cookers on the market, it is important that you choose one to suit your needs. There are certain variables, both in terms of design and price, but slow cookers generally operate on similar principles.

A slow cooker consists of a sturdy, heatproof outer casing and an inner cooking pot into which the food is placed. The outer casing is made of either stainless steel or aluminium and is where the heating element and controls are housed. The inner cooking pot is usually removable. The lid on a slow cooker fits snugly so that heat cannot escape. The condensation that occurs during the slow, low-heat cooking process gathers around the lip of the pot and creates a water seal. The condensation is then released back into the pot and it is this that keeps the food moist. The combination of a long cooking time and the steam that is created within the pot destroys any bacteria, making it a safe cooking method. It is important to resist the temptation to open the lid – this will release heat and break the water seal and you will need to add a further 20 minutes to the cooking time.

Choosing the right shape and size

Slow cookers come in a range of sizes, but small machines start from 1.5 litres (2¾ pints), which is suitable for 1–2 adults; a medium-sized 3.5 litre (6 pint) cooker is great for 4 people; for 6 people or more, choose a 5 litre (8¾ pint) model or larger. However, bigger isn't necessarily better unless you are catering for large numbers or wish to batch cook – you need to half-fill a slow cooker for optimum performance, and accommodate it on your kitchen worktop, so choose wisely. Slow cookers can be either round or oval in shape; the choice is down to personal preference. Casseroles, chillies, and curries are all perfect for round cookers but an oval one is preferable if you wish to cook whole joints of meat or chickens, and fit in pudding basins or ramekins. The removable inner cooking pots are usually ceramic, but they are also available in cast-aluminium. Ceramic pots are easiest to wash, retain the heat well, and can be served straight to the table. Cast-aluminium pots are lighter and allow you to brown food in them first before cooking. Always choose one with a recognized safety mark.

When adapting recipes, bear the following in mind:

- The recipe must contain some liquid if going into the slow cooker.

- If a recipe calls for milk, cream, or soured cream, only add this for the last 30 minutes of cooking. For best results, stir in cream just before serving.

- Make sure all frozen ingredients are thawed and meats are thoroughly defrosted before cooking.

- You may need to reduce spices and herbs, as their flavour becomes concentrated in the slow cooker.

Adapting recipes for the slow cooker

You can easily adapt conventional recipes for the slow cooker. Firstly, find a recipe in this book that is similar in style and has similar ingredients, such as the meat cuts, beans, or vegetables. From this you can ascertain the length of cooking time needed. If you are at worried, leave it to cook for longer – a slow cooker won't boil dry. Secondly, adjust the ingredient quantities to ensure they will all fit in the pot. Finally, as a general guide, halve the liquid in your recipe. This is because the liquid doesn't evaporate in the slow cooker as it does with other methods. You can always top it up if needed, or if you do find yourself with too much, remove the lid and cook on High until the excess liquid has evaporated away.

Using the slow cooker

Slow cookers are more efficient than traditional ovens and can help to reduce your fuel bill as they use minimum electricity. The vast majority of slow cookers have only 2 or 3 heat settings, making them easy to use. For best results, the slow cooker should be at least half full but no more than two-thirds full when cooking.

HEAT SETTINGS

The various slow cooker models have different functions for heat settings, but as a rule they all have Low and High. Preheating the slow cooker before use raises the temperature of the pot before adding the food, but this differs for each slow cooker so read the manufacturer's instructions for your model.

Low: This is the lowest temperature you can cook at and is ideal for leaving food throughout the day or overnight. Cooking times for Low vary between 6 and 12 hours. The food will cook at around 100°C (200°F).

High: This setting is around 150°C (300°F), and in general the food cooks between 3 and 6 hours. As a rule of thumb, the High setting takes half as long as the Low one, so 1 hour on High setting equals 2 hours on Low.

Auto: This setting starts cooking the food on High for 1 hour, then reduces it to the Low temperature for the remainder of the cooking time.

Keep warm: This holds the food at a lower temperature than Low to keep it at an ideal heat for serving. Many cookers switch to this setting automatically once the food is cooked. However, do not leave the food standing in the cooker keeping warm for longer than 1–2 hours.

Useful ingredients and equipment

There are a few ingredients that I always have in stock, no matter what, and as soon as I've used them up, they go right back on my shopping list. These are the ones that add flavour or texture to my cooking and I find myself drawn to them all the time. Likewise, my hero accessories – not entirely essential, but they do make cooking easier and more fun!

Hero ingredients
The ingredients I couldn't be without:

- Garlic-infused olive or rapeseed (canola) oil
- Low-salt stock cubes
- Low-salt soy sauce
- Mushroom powder
- Vanilla extract (not essence)
- Ground cinnamon
- Tomato purée (paste)
- Apple purée pouches
- Cheddar and smoked Cheddar cheese
- Sweet and smoked paprika
- Dried mixed herbs
- Peanut butter – 100% peanut
- Cornflour (cornstarch)

Kitchen essentials
For making life in your kitchen that little bit easier:

- Good set of kitchen knives – a small paring knife for chopping foods like fruit, a large chef's knife for cutting meat and large vegetables, plus a serrated bread knife for cutting anything with a crumb – try to get the best your money can buy and keep them as sharp as you can
- 2 chopping boards, one for cutting vegetables and fruit and another for cutting meat
- Tin opener
- Rolling pin
- Digital weighing scales
- Potato masher
- Wooden spoons
- Rubber or silicone spatula
- Non-metal fish slice
- Colander or wide kitchen spider strainer tool
- Non-metal whisk, or rubber-tipped metal whisk
- Large non-stick frying pan – 28cm (11in) or larger
- Set of lidded saucepans
- Box grater
- Mixing bowls – minimum one small and one large
- Hand stick blender

Tips for success
Choosing the right equipment and using your ingredients with a little know-how will help you achieve great results from slow cooking.

Peppercorns and seeds, such as cumin, coriander, and fennel, are best crushed before adding to the pot so they release their flavour slowly.

For maximum flavour, brown the meat at the start of cooking, and soften aromatic vegetables such as onions and garlic by sautéing

Always add delicate ingredients that don't need much cooking, such as fish and seafood, towards the end of the cooking time.

Moroccan tagines, cone-shaped earthenware cooking pots with tall lids, are apt for slow cooking. They are designed to return condensation back into the dish to keep the food moist. For versatility, choose one that can be used on the hob (with a diffuser) and in the oven.

Woody herbs, such as rosemary and thyme, are robust enough to add at the beginning of cooking; add delicate herbs, such as parsley, towards the end of cooking, or stir into the finished dish.

For traditional slow cooking, choose a thick-walled flameproof casserole that holds the heat well, such as a cast-iron or an enamelled cast-iron one. Ensure it has a well-fitting lid and can be used on the hob or in the oven. Cast-iron casseroles can be heavy, so choose one with two easy-to-hold handles. Pick a size to suit your requirements: as a rule of thumb, food should only reduce down to about three-quarters of the pot's volume once cooked from full.

If topping up the liquid during cooking, add hot liquid to prevent lowering the cooking temperature.

Essential recipe techniques

Slow cooking provides a convenient one-pot cooking method, but with most dishes there are a few stages of cooking that are needed first, such as marinating, browning the meat, or sautéing vegetables. Each of these techniques adds depth of flavour to the finished dish. Deglazing during cooking is vital for enhancing the taste of your sauce, while reducing and thickening are great troubleshooting techniques for thin sauces.

Sautéing
This requires high heat and a good heavy-based pan. Sautéing vegetables before adding them to the slow cooker enables their natural water content to evaporate, thus concentrating their flavour. Heat some oil or butter, add the vegetables to the pan, and cook until they start to caramelize and soften. Always cook the hardest vegetables first as these will take longer.

Browning
This technique caramelizes the natural sugars that are in meat and turns it a golden colour. Browning adds flavour and depth to your dish, so it is worth doing before it is added to the slow cooker. Season the meat and add it to hot oil in a frying pan and cook over a medium-high heat. Leave the meat to cook for a few minutes. When the underside is golden, turn and cook the other side. Remove the meat and set it aside while you prepare the rest of the ingredients. You could dust the meat in seasoned flour before browning, as it helps thicken the consistency of the sauce.

Deglazing
The sauce is all-important as it can make or break the dish. This technique is used often after browning and sautéing and before cooking in the slow cooker. Remove the food from the pan and spoon off excess fat, then deglaze the caramelized juices by adding stock, water, or wine. Stir to loosen the particles and incorporate them into the liquid. Reduce and finish as required.

Reducing and thickening
When a sauce is too thin, it can be either reduced or thickened to improve its flavour and texture. To reduce, turn the heat to HIGH and remove the lid. Add stock and bring to the boil, then boil, uncovered, for 20 minutes to reduce by half. Thickening gives sauces extra body and consistency. Dissolve cornflour (cornstarch) in water and add the mixture to the dish. You could also add a roux – a mixture of flour and water – stirring it into the simmering sauce and cooking to prevent it from turning the sauce lumpy.

Adapting the recipes to suit your diet

If you have specific dietary requirements, whether dairy-free, gluten-free, egg-free, vegan or vegetarian, there are ways to adapt the recipes in this book to suit your family's needs. Look out for the icons below accompanying each recipe to find out if it suits your dietary requirements. Whenever you see a * next to the letters in the dietary icon, this indicates that the recipe can be adapted to suit this dietary requirement. Please take care and turn to this section for possible alternatives to the ingredients listed. Here, I have listed some foods that you can use as substitutes – unless it is specifically stated in the recipe, choose whichever one works best for you. Always check product packets for hidden ingredients you may not be aware of.

GF Gluten free

EF Egg free

DF Dairy free

V Vegetarian

Vg Vegan

DISCLAIMER Those following strict allergen diets should always check the packet for guidance about suitability.

Dairy-free cooking

BUTTER For most recipes, you can replace butter with dairy-free spreads (these are better for baking), or with coconut oil, olive oil, or sunflower oil.

MILK You can substitute dairy milk for a plant-based alternative in all recipes. For under 2s, all milk should be full-fat to ensure little ones are taking enough energy from their food. Soy, pea, and oat milks are all a suitable swap from 6 months onwards. Nut and hemp milks can be served to children over 2 years old, although do bear in mind that these are lower in calories, so not always an ideal staple for young children. Avoid rice milk as this is not suitable for children under the age of 5 years. Try to choose a milk that is fortified with extra vitamins to ramp up the nutritional intake.

CHEESE There are many dairy-free cheeses on the market these days; shop around and find ones which you like the taste of and melt well. It is best to choose a cheese alternative that is fortified with B12 and other vitamins, if possible. Alternatively, in most recipes you can just leave out the cheese or swap it for nutritional yeast flakes (about 1 tablespoon replaces 40–50g/ 1½–2oz of cheese); however, be mindful that in both cases this may reduce a little of the moisture content in the finished dish.

DAIRY CREAM, CREAM CHEESE, AND YOGURT In most supermarkets, you will find plant-based alternatives to these products. If you do struggle to find anything, use an alternative that is a similar texture to what you are trying to replace. For example, you could replace Greek yogurt with plant-based yogurt or plant-based cream cheese thinned down with a little plant-based milk. Experiment and make the recipe suit you.

Egg-free cooking

If egg is the main ingredient in a recipe, for example in an omelette, it is not always possible to replace with an alternative option, and so it may be best to choose another recipe in this case. However, when egg is used to bind ingredients together, such as for pancakes, flax and chia eggs are a great substitute. Be mindful that they do not expand and rise like a hen's egg would, so the results will be a little different; however, they do work to keep the ingredients together and add a little extra moisture to the recipe. To make 1 replacement egg, follow the instructions below, before adding to your recipe.

CHIA EGG Stir 1 tablespoon of chia seeds with 2½ tablespoons of warm water and set aside for 5 minutes.

FLAX EGG Stir 1 tablespoon of ground flax seeds with 3 tablespoons of warm water and set aside for 10–15 minutes.

EGG REPLACERS In recent years, it has become much easier to purchase egg replacers in supermarkets. Look out for either powdered versions or products in the chilled aisle. These are used predominantly in baking.

EGG WASH ALTERNATIVES When a recipe calls for an egg wash, this is to give a little sheen to your bake, especially pastry. Use plant-based milk as a substitute (soy, almond, or coconut milk works best), or aquafaba – the liquid in a can of chickpeas.

Gluten-free cooking

Gluten is the name of a protein found in wheat and some other grains. If you follow a gluten-free diet, there are plenty of alternatives. In most cases, plain (all-purpose) or self-raising flour can be replaced in like-for-like quantities with shop-bought gluten-free variations. Also, look out for gluten-free baking powder, soy sauce, Worcestershire sauce, mustard, and stock cubes, as some of these products may contain traces of gluten. While oats don't contain gluten, they are often processed in factories with other grains that do, so always look for oats marked as "gluten-free" to avoid any cross contamination.

Meat replacement in recipes

VEGGIES You can generally replace meat with either firm vegetables like mushrooms or butternut squash, or meat-replacement products. Just be mindful that meat-replacement products often contain added salt, so factor this in when serving to little ones. They are also usually low in fat; therefore, it is important to replace this lost fat with other forms of higher-calorific foods like avocado or nut butters, especially when serving to babies, as little ones need those extra calories to help them grow.

TOFU This is an excellent meat replacement. Use the correct firmness and follow the instructions on the packet to incorporate it into the recipe. Soft silken tofu is a good substitute for thick cream in desserts or to add at the end of cooking soups, while firm tofu is great to breadcrumb to turn into nuggets or stir through pasta or noodle dishes.

Be mindful that there are hidden traces of meat and fish in some foods like Worcestershire sauce, which usually contains anchovies, so try to find vegetarian options or leave these ingredients out. Some cheeses use animal rennet in their production; however, there are plenty on the market that are vegetarian, and this will be displayed on the packet.

Nut-free cooking

When a recipe calls for peanut butter or crushed nuts, there are options you can take depending on your specific allergies. If possible, opt to substitute for nut-free butters like tahini (sesame seed paste), sunflower, or specific nut-free butters. You could also leave out the nuts altogether; however, please note that nut butters might be added as a binder or for extra moisture, so the end result may differ slightly.

Salt and sugar

All the recipes in this book can be served to every member of your family, including babies aged 6 months and up. The recipes have been developed to be low in salt and sugar so that they are safe for little ones to enjoy but still delicious for us adults too. However, not everyone has the same preference when it comes to seasoning – it's something we learn to get a taste for as we get older. Therefore, please do feel free to season your own food to your taste once the family meal has been dished up, or when your little one's portion has been removed from the pan. Adapt these recipes with extra chilli, pepper, sugar, or spice if you feel like it too. Really make it your own – because food is there to be enjoyed!

A note on vanilla extract

Traditionally, vanilla extract is made using alcohol, which you might not feel comfortable offering to little ones in its raw form. If you are adding vanilla extract to a recipe that will be cooked or baked, the quantity that ends up in the final dish is so small that all traces of alcohol will be removed in the cooking process. These days, you can buy alcohol-free vanilla extract, and this is particularly useful for no-cook recipes or if your dietary requirements don't allow any alcohol. Avoid using vanilla essence (instead of extract), as this is essentially synthetic vanilla and not ideal for little ones.

SALT INTAKE GUIDE

- Babies under 12 months should have less than 1g salt per day (0.4g sodium)

- Toddlers aged 1–3 years should have a maximum of 2g salt per day (0.8g sodium)

- Children aged 4–6 years should have a maximum of 3g salt per day (1.2g sodium)

- Children aged 7–10 years should have a maximum of 5g salt per day (2g sodium)

- Children aged 11 years plus and adults should have a maximum of 6g salt per day (2.4g sodium)

Foods to avoid for little ones

SATURATED FAT Try to limit your child's intake of saturated fat in foods like cakes, cookies, and crisps (potato chips). Babies and young children need lots of healthy fats, so choose full-fat versions of milk or cheese.

SUGAR Try to avoid too many sugary treats, including naturally occurring sugars in foods like fresh fruit juices, as over-exposure to sweet tastes can lead to a preference for sugary flavours and tooth decay.

HONEY Honey can contain bacteria that can produce toxins in baby's intestines leading to infant botulism, which is a very serious illness. Avoid serving honey to babies under the age of 12 months.

RAW EGGS From 6 months, you can serve eggs to baby. In the UK, choose hen's eggs that have the British Lion quality stamp on them. If the eggs are not British Lion stamped, always cook the eggs until they are solid.

SOY SAUCE This is normally very high in salt and is not recommended. Choose a low-salt soy sauce, but be careful as each brand is different.

WHOLE NUTS Avoid serving whole nuts and peanuts to babies and children under the age of 5 years as they are a choking hazard. Nut butters, crushed nuts, and ground nuts can be served from around the age of 6 months.

CERTAIN CHEESES It is advised to offer pasteurized full-fat cheese from the age of 6 months. There is a risk of the bacteria listeria in soft cheese like Brie, Camembert, ripened goat's cheese, or blue cheese, but you can use these cheeses to cook with, as the listeria is killed during cooking.

RICE DRINKS Babies and children up to the age of 5 years, should not drink rice-based drinks as they contain high levels of arsenic. Babies are fine to eat rice, as the levels are monitored in the EU for rice and rice products.

RAW SHELLFISH Always fully cook shellfish such as mussels, oysters, clams, and cockles to avoid the risk of food poisoning.

Storage and freezing guidelines

Storing and freezing food safely is important. It really comes down to how and when you package up the food to determine when and for how long you can store it. For specific instructions for each recipe within this book, look out for the "Love your leftovers" section of each recipe.

How to store food in the fridge

Ensure you always put leftover food in airtight containers when storing in the fridge. This not only slows down the growth of bacteria, but helps to stop other food flavours leaching into all the food in your fridge.

Always fully cool food before putting it in the fridge. Putting hot or warm food in the fridge adjusts the temperature of your fridge and therefore compromises the other food you are storing.

Try to cool food as quickly as possible by spreading on a cool surface before chilling. Ideally cool within 2 hours – however, if you are storing rice, ensure it is fully cooled and refrigerated within 1 hour of cooking.

A general rule of thumb is that most leftover cooked food will last for 2 days in the fridge. However, some more perishable foods will only last for 24 hours; for example, cooked fish.

Always store raw meat on a separate shelf from fresh fruit and veg.

How to store food in the freezer

Ensure you package up all foods in airtight containers or bags to prevent freezer burn.

Try to freeze in portions so you only need to defrost what you need.

Label and date the food you put in the freezer so you can ensure you aren't keeping it for longer than is safe.

Always store frozen raw meat on a different shelf to frozen fruit and veg, as the veggies may be eaten uncooked.

Reheating leftover chilled food

Some food can be eaten cold after storing in the fridge or defrosting, as long as it was fully cooked beforehand. Fruit like berries can be eaten uncooked after defrosting. However, if you choose to reheat the food, you must ensure that it is completely piping hot before cooling and serving. It can be tempting to heat just a little, especially if serving to little ones – however, this is dangerous as bacteria risk increases at this temperature.

Keeping food cold under 8°C means the bacteria is at dormant level, and is safe to consume, or heat food to over 70°C "piping hot", to kill off the bacteria in the food. You can then cool the food to a safe warm temperature to feed to your little one. Don't forget to ensure your fridge is always at 5°C or less to ensure food is stored at a safe temperature too.

Reheating frozen food

Generally the best advice is to fully defrost food in the fridge before reheating and serving. However, some food can be cooked straight from frozen, which saves on time.

If you defrost food at room temperature, keep an eye on when it is defrosted and place it in the fridge straight away – storing defrosted food at room temperature for prolonged periods of time can compromise the safety of that food.

Foods that are raw inside need to be defrosted first, as the outside will cook and burn before the inside has had a chance to do so.

Batch cooking

My favourite kind of recipe is one that will feed you now and also again on another day. Batch cooking can help you save time in the kitchen and keep costs down on ingredients while making sure you still have a stock of delicious, nutritious meals on hand when you're at your busiest.

Utilize your slow cooker for batch cooking. It's easy to make a large portion in your slow cooker, which is perfect for storing away leftovers. You can also make up slow cooker freezer dump bags where you prepare all the ingredients for the slow cooker, place in a freezer-safe bag and freeze for a later date. Great to do a couple at a time. Then defrost overnight and, in the morning, simply add to a slow cooker. When you get home later, dinner is ready, easy peasy!

How to reduce food waste

Unused and uneaten leftover cooked meals are one of the biggest contributors to food waste. It's very easy to cook too much food, to store it with the best intentions to eat it another day, but for whatever reason that does not happen. Here are my top tips for reducing food waste.

FRUIT BOWL ROULETTE Do you find fruit in your fruit bowl is often going off before you have a chance to eat it? It might be worth storing those bananas elsewhere, as bananas release a gas called ethene which speeds up the ripening of other fruits. Equally, if you have a hard piece of fruit you wish to ripen quicker, put a few bananas on top and it'll help you along.

GET HERBY! Don't let your garlic and herbs go to waste. Chop them up finely and add to a freezer bag to use on their own, adding to any recipe you please. Or you can add them to a little bit of oil to make a flavourful accompaniment to any meal. Unsterilized containers of simple olive oil and herbs mixed together will last in the fridge for up to 2 weeks.

ARE YOU COOL ENOUGH? Check whether your fridge is cool enough, just a few degrees too warm could mean your milk is turning sour quicker or your veggies are softening faster. It should be between 0–5°C.

CHILL YOUR BREAD In the UK, we don't often store our bread in the fridge, let alone in the freezer, but it can help to maximize its shelf life. Perfect for loaves you plan to toast anyway! If you're not keen on this idea, chop stale leftover bread into small croutons, bake in a low oven until completely dried, then pulse in a food processor to your desired consistency. Store in an airtight container for 2 months in a cool, dark place, or freeze for 6 months.

DON'T BE AFRAID TO SWITCH THINGS UP If you could only get a larger amount of food than you expected, try to incorporate this into your meal plan to avoid leftovers going to waste.

FREEZE THOSE SCRAPS! Instead of throwing away vegetable and potato peelings, ensure the veg is clean before peeling, then store those scraps in a bag in the freezer. Keep adding to the bag whenever you have some scraps, then when the bag is full you can make a delicious soup, or blend it and add to stews for an extra veggie hit.

STICK TO THE PLAN! Shop according to your meal plan and shopping list.

Keeping kids entertained

We all know how tricky it can be to get the kids to settle sometimes, especially when you need it most! So please don't feel guilty for using the TV or tablet to keep them occupied for a few moments – parent in the way that works for you to keep your sanity! When you have the time and patience, and the kids need a break from the screen, here are a few ideas that you may find helpful to keep them entertained. Of course, please keep in mind the age of your child for each of these, as some items, such as small objects, may not be suitable for smaller children.

Stuff an array of multicoloured pom-poms into a large whisk and let baby try to pick them out!

Tape small objects like toys, hollow balls, baby cutlery, etc. to baby's high chair tray. It'll keep them occupied for a few moments.

Make a sensory basket filled with kitchen items for baby to play with so they can feel involved with what you're doing. Include items like a metal whisk, a wooden spoon, or a smash-proof bowl.

Turn a colander upside down and stick lots of craft feathers into a bunch of the holes; baby can pull them out and enjoy the soft sensory experience.

Make up a cooking activity bag or basket and attach it to the high chair or stash it near to where you cook. This way, there are always toys on hand to keep the little one occupied while you're distracted for 10 minutes.

My Nina has always loved a sticker sheet, which keeps her entertained for a little bit. My top tip is to peel away the sticker sheet from the edges, leaving the actual stickers still attached to the backing. This way, your little ones can pick off the stickers themselves more easily.

Let little ones enjoy food that isn't filling but takes a long time to eat. Like a bowl of pomegranate seeds, rice cakes, small pieces of cereal or cooked cold peas. Baby will spend lots of time practising their pincer grip. This one is especially good when you are eating out and waiting for the food to arrive.

Soups & Stews

Leek and potato soup	26
Hearty goulash soup	29
Hidden veg tomato soup	30
Mexican soup	33
Proper beef stew and dumplings	35
Tomato and spinach fish stew	36
Spanish chicken and sweetcorn stew	38
Freezer raid veg stew	41
Smoky pork and bean stew	42
Turkish chicken stew	45
Easy aubergine stew	46
Dump and bake bread	49

From a classic Leek and potato soup to a hearty Smoky pork and bean stew, all the recipes in this chapter are perfect for when you want to make an easy and nutritious meal. I've even included a bread that you can bake in the slow cooker to accompany the dishes.

Leek and potato soup

This classic soup is easy to whip up in the morning for a warming and hearty lunch or dinner on a cold winter's day. Make it into a substantial meal by serving it with fresh crusty bread and butter.

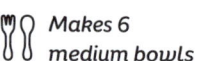

Makes 6 medium bowls

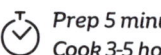

Prep 5 minutes, Cook 3-5 hours

Ingredients

350g (12oz) all-rounder potatoes

2 medium leeks

1 low-salt vegetable or chicken stock cube*

2 garlic cloves

freshly ground black pepper

150ml (⅔ cup) milk*

2 heaped tbsp full-fat cream cheese or crème fraîche*

Peel and cube the potatoes into 2cm (¾in) chunks and add to the slow cooker pot.

Slice the leeks down the centre, keeping the stalk attached, then run water from the tap through the leeks with the open side down, so that any dirt washes away. Then roughly chop the leeks into chunks, discarding the stalk and adding to the slow cooker pot.

Crumble in the stock cube, peel the garlic cloves and chop in half, then add to the slow cooker along with a generous grinding of black pepper.

Measure the milk into a jug and add to the slow cooker, then measure in 1 litre (4¼ cups) of water, adding this too. Give everything a really good stir, then put the lid on. Cook for 3 hours on HIGH or for 5 hours on LOW. It'll be done when the potatoes are fork tender.

Blitz to a smooth consistency using a stick blender. Now add the cream cheese and stir to melt into the soup. You can thin it down if you wish with a little more milk.

Serve as is with a little crusty buttered bread for dunking.

 Love your leftovers

Leftovers will keep for 2 days in the fridge, or freeze for 1 month. Defrost thoroughly and reheat in a saucepan until bubbling and piping hot throughout.

Hearty goulash soup

 GF*
 EF
DF*

Having a Hungarian background, goulash to me has always been a family favourite soup. A hearty, comforting broth packed full of goodness with deliciously succulent meat, tender potatoes, and soft peppers that just melt into the sauce.

 Serves 2 adults and 2 littles

 Prep 10 minutes, Cook 4 hours

Ingredients

1 tbsp sunflower oil

1 large onion, finely diced

1 tsp caraway seeds (optional)

600–700g (1lb 5oz–1lb 9oz) diced stewing beef or lamb shoulder

1 red pepper

1 yellow pepper

2 large carrots

6 fresh tomatoes, quartered, or 1 x 400g (14oz) can of chopped tomatoes

3 garlic cloves, finely diced

2 tsp dried mixed herbs

3 tbsp sweet, mild paprika

2 fresh or dried bay leaves

2 low-salt beef stock cubes*

1 tbsp cornflour (cornstarch)

350g (12oz) potatoes (I prefer new potatoes as they hold together well, but an all-rounder like Maris Piper will do)

Heat a teaspoon of the oil in a large heavy-based frying pan over a low heat. Add the onion and soften for 2 minutes (see p12), then add the caraway seeds, if using, and cook for a further 2 minutes. Once translucent, add the onion and seeds to the slow cooker pot.

Return the pan to the heat and crank up the temperature to high. Add the remaining oil, then fry the diced meat until browned and caramelized on the edges. Add to the slow cooker pot.

Deseed the peppers and cut into 1cm (½in) wide strips, or finely dice if your little ones prefer (not "bits", as my Nina calls them). Peel and cut the carrots into 2.5cm (1in) chunks. Add both to the slow cooker with the tomatoes, garlic, herbs, 2 tablespoons of the paprika, and the bay leaves, then crumble in the stock cubes.

Once all the beef is added to the slow cooker, deglaze the pan to extract as much flavour as possible – add 300ml (1¼ cups) of boiling water to the pan and use a wooden spoon to scrape any crispy bits from the bottom, then add this liquid to the slow cooker. Stir really well, cover, and cook for 2 hours on HIGH.

Once the 2 hours is up, add the remaining paprika, the cornflour, and a little cold water to a small bowl and mix to make a runny paste. Peel and dice the potatoes into 2.5cm (1in) chunks. Stir the goulash gently, then add 400–500ml (1⅔–generous 2 cups) of boiling water (depending on how soupy you like it). Add the cornflour paste and potatoes and stir. Pop the lid on and cook for 2 hours on HIGH.

Serve in deep bowls with sour cream and crusty bread. Adults, this is delicious as is, but you can add a sprinkling of salt, if you like.

 Love your leftovers

The soup can be kept for 2 days, or frozen for up to 3 months. Reheat in a saucepan on the hob until piping hot throughout.

Hidden veg tomato soup

This vibrant soup is bursting with flavour and is packed with lots of brightly coloured veggies. The kids will willingly gobble it all up! Garnish with a sprig of basil and serve with freshy crusty bread for dunking.

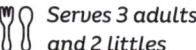
Serves 3 adults and 2 littles

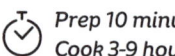
Prep 10 minutes, Cook 3-9 hours

Ingredients

1 red or yellow pepper, deseeded and roughly chopped

4 celery sticks, roughly chopped

2 leeks, slit open and washed, roughly chopped

3 garlic cloves, peeled

1 low-salt chicken or vegetable stock cube*

2 tsp dried mixed herbs

2 heaped tsp smoked paprika

1 tbsp light soft brown sugar (optional)

1 x 260g (11oz) can of unsalted sweetcorn in water

3 x 400g (14oz) cans of peeled plum tomatoes in tomato juice

freshly ground black pepper

fresh basil leaves, to garnish (optional)

Add the roughly chopped pepper, celery, and leeks to the slow cooker pot along with the peeled garlic. Crumble in the stock cube, add the dried herbs, smoked paprika, and sugar, if using. Add the entire can of sweetcorn, including the water, and a good grinding of black pepper.

Empty the cans of tomatoes into the slow cooker, then fill them each with a small amount of tap water – no more than a quarter of the can – and swill out any remaining tomato, pouring the liquid into the slow cooker pot too. Stir very well and pop the lid on to cook for a minimum of 3 hours on HIGH or up to 8–9 hours on LOW. This recipe is a good one if you will be out all day and want to come home to a dinner that's ready.

Once the veggies are soft, simply blend using a stick blender until smooth. The soup is now ready to serve in bowls topped with black pepper and fresh basil leaves to garnish, if you wish. Adults may like a tiny pinch of extra sugar and a little salt for added seasoning.

If you have time, I prefer to add an extra step and sieve this soup to remove any pulp – the kiddos may prefer it this way too (the soup has not been sieved for this recipe photo). Add a touch of boiling water if you'd prefer to thin down the soup to perfect bread dunking consistency, or keep it thick to serve with pasta.

If you would like to adapt this dish into a delicious hidden veggie pasta sauce, skip the step of adding water to the tomato cans and drain the sweetcorn can before adding it to the slow cooker. This way the finished sauce will be much thicker and better for coating your pasta – perfect with a little grated cheese, too.

♡ Love your leftovers

Leftovers will keep for up to 2–3 days in the fridge, or freeze for up to 4 months. Add to a saucepan to melt and reheat until bubbling.

Mexican soup

GF*

EF

DF*

V*

Vg*

Fully loaded, this taco-inspired soup is bursting with flavour and goodness. Super easy to whip up, and comforting enough for a cosy winter's day, but easily freshened up for those warmer months with some fresh toppings to enjoy on the side.

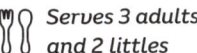

Serves 3 adults and 2 littles

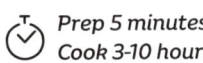

Prep 5 minutes, Cook 3-10 hours

Ingredients

500g (1lb 2oz) lean minced (ground) beef* or plant-based mince*

1 x 400g (14oz) can of kidney beans in water

2 small onions

2 x 400g (14oz) cans of chopped tomatoes

1 low-salt beef or vegetable stock cube*

300g (10½oz) frozen sweetcorn

2 tsp smoked paprika

2 tsp ground cumin

3 crushed garlic cloves or 3 tsp garlic granules

freshly ground black pepper

To serve

grated cheese*

sour cream or yogurt*

bread or tortilla chips*

Add the beef to a large non-stick frying pan set over a high heat. Break it up and cook for 5 minutes. You can either leave the meat in decent-sized chunks (around a 50p coin size) or break up the meat very small with a wooden spoon as it browns (see p12).

Meanwhile, prepare the rest of the soup. Drain and rinse the kidney beans and add to the slow cooker pot. If your little ones are under 2, I recommend smashing them a little to break the beans into smaller pieces. Do this with a potato masher in the slow cooker pot.

Now add the tomatoes, then fill each can with cold water, swilling any residue into the water, and add this to the slow cooker too. Crumble in the stock cube, followed by the remaining ingredients.

Once the mince has browned all over and you see no raw red meat, add this to the slow cooker too, including any juices. Mix everything really well and put the lid on.

This is a great one to have simmering away all day while you're out so cook for 8–10 hours on LOW, or if you need it done quicker, 3–4 hours on HIGH will be fine too.

Once done, serve as is with some grated cheese on top, and some sour cream, if you like. Bread or tortilla chips are great for dunking and scooping.

Adults, give your portion a really good seasoning with salt, and if you're serving to little ones under 12 months, I recommend blending their portion to a chunky texture so it's easier to eat. Alternatively, drain the liquid from the soup and serve this in a cup, and the other ingredients on the side with a spoon.

 Love your leftovers

Leftovers will keep for 3 days in the fridge, or freeze for up to 3 months. Defrost and reheat until piping hot in the microwave or saucepan.

Proper beef stew and dumplings

A hug in a bowl on a cold, rainy day. The best thing about beef stew is the smell that fills your house throughout the day. The anticipation brings me so much joy! Be sure to brown the meat as it locks in so much flavour and adds depth to the final dish.

 Serves 2 adults and 3 littles

 Prep 20 minutes, Cook 4–8 hours

Ingredients

5 celery sticks

1 medium brown onion

3 small carrots

2 tbsp sunflower oil

750g (1lb 10oz) lean diced stewing beef

2 tbsp plain (all-purpose) flour*

2 large potatoes

1 tbsp Worcestershire sauce (optional)

2 fresh or dried bay leaves

3 garlic cloves, minced

1 tsp dried mixed herbs

2 low-salt beef stock cubes*

freshly ground black pepper

For the dumplings

200g (1⅔ cups) self-raising flour*, plus extra for dusting

70g (2½oz) beef or vegetarian suet*

50g (1¾oz) Cheddar cheese*, finely grated

Finely dice the celery, onion, and carrots. Add all this veg to a large heavy-based frying pan with a little drizzle of the oil, and cook for around 5 minutes until the vegetables have started to soften (see p.12). Stir occasionally to ensure they cook evenly.

Meanwhile, on a plate, coat the beef in the flour and shake off any excess. Set aside. Peel and quarter the potatoes.

Transfer the softened veg to your slow cooker pot and put the empty frying pan back on the hob over a high heat with a little more oil. Brown the meat in the pan in batches, making sure it has plenty of room, until the outside is dark brown with crispy edges, but the inside is still raw (see p.12). Transfer to the slow cooker.

Meanwhile, add the remaining ingredients and a generous grind of black pepper to the slow cooker. In a large jug, mix the stock cubes with 800ml (3½ cups) of boiling water until fully dissolved, and add this liquid to the slow cooker too. Stir well, then pop the lid on. Cook for 6–8 hours on LOW, or for 4–5 hours on HIGH, until the meat is tender and falls apart with gentle pressure.

This is delicious as it is; however, if you're like me and love a thick and hearty stew, 1 hour before it's ready, add dumplings. To make these, measure all the ingredients into a bowl, season with black pepper, and give it a stir. Trickle in enough cold water to make a slightly sticky, mouldable dough – about 160ml (generous ⅔ cup).

Stir the stew well and keep the lid off. Flour your hands, then take a small amount of the dough and roll it in your hands gently to form a golf-ball-sized dumpling. Plop it into the stew and repeat with the rest – the dough should make around 10 dumplings. If your dough is too sticky, use a spoon to dollop the mixture into the stew, or add a touch more flour until it's dry enough to handle.

Add the dumplings neatly without overlapping each other, then put the lid on and cook on HIGH until they have doubled in size. Try not to take the lid off as this will affect their rise. The anticipation for the final reveal is worth the wait!

Tomato and spinach fish stew

GF*
EF
DF*

When I think of slow cooker meals, fish doesn't usually come to mind. However, this dish gives you soft and flaky delicate fish in a rich, flavourful tomato and spinach sauce. As a bonus, this recipe calls for frozen fish cooked straight from the freezer, which is such an easy and economical way of adding fish to our diet.

Serves 2 adults and 2 littles

Prep 5 minutes, Cook 3-7 hours

Ingredients

500g (1lb 2oz) crushed tomatoes or passata (strained tomatoes)

8 cubes of chopped frozen spinach

1 x 400g (14oz) can of coconut milk

2 tsp sweet paprika

2 tsp smoked paprika

1 tsp dried mixed herbs

2 tsp garlic granules or 2 garlic cloves, minced

2 tbsp tomato purée (paste)

1 tsp sugar (optional)

1 low-salt chicken or vegetable stock cube*, crumbled

4–6 frozen skinless and boneless large white fish fillets, e.g. haddock, bass, pollock, or cod

Add the crushed tomatoes or passata to the slow cooker pot along with the frozen spinach, coconut milk, sweet and smoked paprika, dried herbs, garlic granules or fresh garlic, tomato purée, sugar, if using, and crumbled stock cube. Give it all a really good stir so that there are no lumps apart from the frozen spinach, which will defrost as it cooks. Pop the lid on and cook on HIGH for 3 hours or on LOW for 5–6 hours.

The smell in your kitchen will be divine when the cooking time is up. Give the sauce another good stir so that any small lumps of stock cube that have melted during cooking are distributed evenly through the sauce.

Now, take the fish out of the freezer and add the frozen fillets to the sauce. Stir and make sure each fillet is submerged in the sauce, then put the lid back on and cook for a further 30–40 minutes on HIGH or 50–60 minutes on LOW, or until the fish flakes easily, as this will tell you that it's done. To double check, lift up one fish fillet gently using a fish slice, then gently flake it in half at its thickest point. Place your finger on the white fish flesh inside, if it's too hot to keep your finger there for a few seconds, then it's done. If it feels just lukewarm, you need to cook it for another 10–20 minutes until piping hot.

Serve alongside some rice to soak up the sauce or crusty bread for dipping.

 Love your leftovers

This dish is best served fresh; however, if you have any leftovers, these will keep for up to 24 hours in the fridge. To reheat, place in an ovenproof dish, cover with foil and heat in a hot oven for 10–15 minutes until piping hot throughout. You can also freeze any leftovers for up to 1 month. Defrost in the fridge and then reheat as above.

Family fish
The fish fillets will shrink a little when cooked, so for a hungry family of 4 I recommend cooking 6 fillets.

Spanish chicken and sweetcorn stew

Soft tender chicken, sweetcorn kernels, in a delicious smoky paprika sauce, this is fantastic paired with potatoes, pasta, or rice, or just on its own with little soft flatbreads for dunking. Garnish with a sprinkling of finely chopped herbs, if you like.

 Serves 3 adults and 2 littles

 Prep 5 minutes, Cook 3-6 hours

Ingredients

1 x 400g (14oz) can of cannellini or haricot beans in water

500g (1lb 2oz) boneless chicken thighs

300g (10½oz) frozen sweetcorn kernels

500g (1lb 2oz) passata (strained tomatoes)

3 tsp smoked paprika

1 low-salt chicken stock cube*

2 large garlic cloves, crushed

good grinding of black pepper

Rinse the beans in the sink, then add to a flat-bottomed bowl and mash using a potato masher. It doesn't need to be smooth, but make sure you smush every bean so none are left whole. Add them to the slow cooker pot along with the rest of the ingredients. Half-fill the passata container with cold water from the tap, swilling out any left in the corners and add this too.

Give it all a really good stir, ensuring the chicken is flattened out too. Then pop the lid on and cook on HIGH for 3 hours or on LOW for 5–6 hours until the chicken is very tender.

Whole sweetcorn kernels do not pose a choking risk to weaning babies, so these are fine to serve whole from 6 months old, but if you're worried, you can blend the sauce a little, keeping some chunks of chicken aside for baby for finger foods. Adults, add a good sprinkling of salt to your portion and some chilli if you fancy it.

 Love your leftovers

Leftovers will keep for 2 days in an airtight container in the fridge, or freeze for up to 3 months. Defrost thoroughly, then either reheat in a saucepan or microwave for 3–4 minutes until piping hot throughout.

Freezer raid veg stew

This a real store-cupboard/freezer winner for when you don't have much in. I always have a packet of chorizo in my fridge, but if you don't or you don't eat meat, then feel free to just leave it out. Equally, feel free to swap out the veg for what you have in; this is a very forgiving recipe and a great one for adapting.

Serves 3 adults and 3 littles

Prep 5 minutes, Cook 3-8 hours

Ingredients

1 x 400g (14oz) can of haricot beans in water

1 x 400g (14oz) can of finely chopped tomatoes or passata

250g (9oz) frozen green beans

250g (9oz) frozen peas

300g (10½oz) frozen sweetcorn

75g (2½oz) mild Spanish chorizo*

4 garlic cloves

1 low-salt chicken or vegetable stock cube*

2 tsp smoked paprika

Rinse the beans and add to the slow cooker pot along with the tomatoes. Fill the empty tomato can with water from the tap and add this too, followed by all the frozen veg.

Peel the chorizo and cut in half lengthways, then into little half-moon discs. Peel the garlic, but leave it whole or chop very roughly. Add these to the veg, along with a crumbled stock cube and the smoked paprika. Give it a very good stir, pop the lid on, and cook on HIGH for 3–4 hours or LOW for 6–8 hours.

Serve in a big bowl with some crusty bread for mopping up all those yummy juices. For little ones under 2, chop the chorizo into smaller pieces for them. If you wish, you can also blend for young newly weaning babies to enjoy on a spoon, or even mix through pasta for a delicious alternative way to enjoy lots of veggies.

 Love your leftovers

Leftovers will store in the fridge for 2 days or freeze for 3 months. Reheat in a saucepan until bubbling and piping hot throughout.

Smoky pork and bean stew

GF*
EF
DF*

Make your home smell amazing all day with this warming slow-cooked recipe. The aroma invites you to dig right into this bowl of comforting goodness. Serve this stew either on its own or with some fresh crusty bread.

Serves 2 adults and 3 littles

Prep 10 minutes, Cook 4-7 hours

Ingredients

1 tbsp garlic-infused oil approx.

500g (1lb 2oz) pork loin or belly, cut into 2.5cm (1in) chunks

2 tbsp plain (all-purpose) flour*

3 x 400g (14oz) cans of mixed beans in water

1 low-salt chicken stock cube*

1 tbsp Worcestershire sauce (optional)

1 tbsp tomato purée (paste)

1 tsp dried mixed herbs

2 tsp garlic granules or 2 garlic cloves, crushed

2 tbsp smoked paprika

400g (14oz) carrots, peeled and cut into large chunks

freshly ground black pepper

Get a large, non-stick frying pan over a medium-high heat and add the garlic oil. Put the kettle on to boil.

Meanwhile, toss the meat in the plain flour, then add to the hot frying pan. Sear the meat on all sides, trying not to touch it too much as this will slow down the caramelization which brings out all the flavour (see p.12).

Add the cans of beans (including the water) to the slow cooker pot. Crumble the stock cube into one of the empty bean cans, then carefully quarter-fill the can with boiling water out of the kettle. Stir to dissolve the stock cube, then add the liquid to the slow cooker along with the Worcestershire sauce, tomato purée, dried herbs, garlic granules or fresh garlic, smoked paprika, carrots, and a generous grinding of black pepper.

Once the meat has turned golden on all sides, add this too and give everything a good stir. Pop the lid on and cook on HIGH for 4 hours or on LOW for 6–7 hours, or until the meat is falling apart and the stew is thick and oozy.

Serve in big bowls with a chunk of bread for dipping.

A note on beans You can use any canned beans you fancy for this recipe (cannellini, pinto, borlotti, black beans, kidney beans, etc.). Just ensure they are in water and not brine, and there is no added salt. You can mix and match beans – you can't go wrong here.

♡ Love your leftovers

Leftovers can be kept for up to 3 days in the fridge or frozen for up to 3 months. Reheat in a saucepan until bubbling and piping hot throughout. Defrost thoroughly before reheating in the same way if you have frozen the stew.

Choosing your pork
When buying the pork, try to find a good ratio of meat to fat. You want a little fat as this gives lots of flavour and juiciness; however, if there's too much fat, this will all melt away during cooking and your stew will be left a little meatless.

Serving to little ones
You can either serve this dish chunky or mash the veggies and potato into the flavourful sauce to enjoy on a spoon.

Turkish chicken stew

This dish is one to cook when it's a little miserable outside, the kids are playing, and you have 10 minutes to prep dinner. Then you can enjoy those delicious smells coming from the kitchen for the whole afternoon. There's soft potatoes, tender chicken, and chunks of courgette and aubergine, which just melt into the sauce, so any picky eaters may be fooled of their presence completely.

Serves 2 adults and 2 littles

Prep 10 minutes, Cook 4–7 hours

Ingredients

1 low-salt chicken stock cube*

700g (1lb 9oz) all-rounder potatoes

1 large courgette (zucchini)

1 large aubergine (eggplant)

3 tsp sweet paprika

2 tsp ground turmeric

2 tsp minced or crushed garlic

1½ tsp ground cumin

1½ tsp dried oregano

6 boneless, skinless chicken thighs

freshly ground black pepper

Crumble the stock cube into a jug, then add 600ml (2½ cups) of boiling water from the kettle. Stir until the stock cube has dissolved, then set aside.

Peel the potatoes and cut them into approx. 2cm (¾in) cubes. Using a vegetable peeler, peel the courgette, then cut it into batons. Chop each baton into approx. 1.5cm (⅝in) chunks. Using a paring knife (because it's a little tricky using the veg peeler), remove the skin of the aubergine as thinly as you can, trying to avoid removing any of the white flesh. Chop the aubergine up into the same size pieces as the courgette.

Add all the chopped veggies to the slow cooker pot along with the paprika, turmeric, garlic, cumin, oregano, and a little black pepper. Add the whole chicken thighs, unfolding them if they have been bunched up inside the packet. Pour the stock into the slow cooker pot and give everything a really good stir.

Pop the lid on and cook on HIGH for 4 hours or on LOW for 6–7 hours, or until the chicken is tender and falls apart easily.

Serve in big bowls, with a little bread for dipping, if you wish. This dish is delicious as it is, but adults may prefer a little salt on their portion to bring out the flavours even more.

♡ Love your leftovers

Leftovers will keep in the fridge for up to 2 days. Reheat in a saucepan until everything is piping hot throughout, especially the chicken. You can also freeze the stew for up to 3 months. Defrost at room temperature before reheating as above.

Easy aubergine stew

This satisfying aubergine stew has smoky, nutty flavour vibes, which remind me of a traditional baba ganoush dip. Serve with rice, bread for dunking, or coated over pasta – delicious!

 Serves 2 adults and 2 littles

Prep 10 minutes, Cook 4-7 hours

Ingredients

2 large aubergines (eggplants)

1 x 400g (14oz) can of crushed tomatoes

1 low-salt vegetable or chicken stock cube*

1 tsp sugar or honey* for over 1s (optional)

1 tbsp tomato purée (paste)

2 tsp dried mixed herbs

15g (½oz) dried porcini mushrooms

2 tsp ground cumin

2 tsp smoked paprika

1 tsp sesame oil

a little freshly ground black pepper

sesame seeds, to serve (optional)

I find this dish is best if you peel the aubergines, but it's not necessary. To peel, I recommend using a sharp paring knife to very thinly slice the skin off the outside, being careful to avoid removing too much of the aubergine flesh. Whether you've peeled them or not, cut the aubergines into cubes, approx. 2cm (¾in) in size – no need to be precise as we'll mash it all later.

Add the cubed aubergine to the slow cooker pot, followed by the can of tomatoes. Fill up the empty can with cold tap water and swill it round to catch any remaining tomato, then add this to the slow cooker too. Crumble the stock cube into the slow cooker, before adding all the remaining ingredients, apart from the sesame oil and sesame seeds. Give it all a good stir, then press all the aubergine chunks down into the liquid. Pop the lid on the slow cooker and cook on HIGH for 4 hours, or LOW for 6–7 hours.

Once the stew is done and the aubergine is super tender, add the sesame oil and use a potato masher to break down the chunks of aubergine (as pictured in the small bowl). Stir everything together so that the mashed aubergine gives the stew a thick, luscious consistency. Alternatively, you can leave it chunky, if you prefer (as pictured in the larger bowl). Serve with a sprinkling of sesame seeds, if you wish.

If serving to little ones, note that even though the dried mushrooms will have rehydrated and softened, babas may still find them tricky to chew, so you can remove these from their portion. Alternatively, pop their portion onto a clean chopping board and run a sharp knife over it, or whizz in a food processor.

 Love your leftovers

Leftovers will keep for up to 2 days in the fridge. Reheat in a saucepan, with an extra splash of water if needed, until piping hot throughout. The stew will also keep in the freezer for up to 3 months. Defrost and then reheat as above.

Dump and bake bread

GF* EF DF* V Vg*

A take on the slow-cooker favourite dump cake, I give you dump and bake bread! This is the perfect thing to easily whip up when you don't have any bread in, delicious for an open sarnie, or serve warm with your favourite soup.

Makes 1 medium loaf

Prep 5 minutes, Cook 2¼ hours

Ingredients

500g (4 cups) plain (all-purpose) flour*

20g (1½ tbsp) baking powder*

100g (3½oz) Cheddar cheese*, grated, plus extra for sprinkling

2 tsp garlic granules

200ml (scant 1 cup) Greek yogurt*

200ml (scant 1 cup) milk*

Take a piece of non-stick baking paper which is large enough to fill your slow cooker pot. Scrunch it up into a bowl in your hands, then unravel it – this will make it easier to mould it into shape in your slow cooker pot.

Now, in a mixing bowl, add the flour and baking powder, sifting it if you feel it is clumpy. Mix together well, then add the cheese and garlic granules and stir again. Now measure in the yogurt and milk and stir with a spoon until it clumps together in parts. Tip the entire lot into your slow cooker, then, with one hand, gently press together to form a round loaf, this should only take a couple of seconds.

Flatten with the palm of your hand to around 5cm (2in) thick, then, using a large sharp knife, cut a cross over the entire loaf, cutting halfway through the dough.

Sprinkle a small handful of cheese over the top. Then take 4 sheets of kitchen paper, ensuring they are all still attached. Fold in half so you have 2 layers of 2 sheets, then place over your slow cooker pot, placing the lid down so that the kitchen paper pokes up all around the lid. This will catch the condensation from the bread, stopping it from going soggy.

Pop the lid on and bake on HIGH for 2 hours and 15 minutes. After this time is up, take the lid off, and remove the paper carefully, ensuring any water gathered doesn't fall onto the loaf. The bread should be a golden brown colour and risen well. Insert a knife into it; if no raw dough comes out onto the blade, it is ready. Remove, using the paper to lift it up, and allow to cool before slicing when still a touch warm – this is when it's tastiest, in my opinion.

♡ Love your leftovers

Leftovers will keep for 3 days in an airtight container, but like normal bread it will start to go stale after the first day, so is best eaten fresh. You can also freeze it for up to 3 months – freeze in slices, then defrost and warm up in the toaster. Or keep in a large loaf and defrost at room temperature.

Pasta

Pork and apple orzotto	54
Meatballs in tomato sauce	56
Chicken Kyiv pasta	61
Butter chicken pasta	62
Traditional Bolognese	65
Spag bol mac and cheese	67
Hodgepodge shortcut lasagne	68
Creamy butternut squash pasta	71
Ricotta and tuna stuffed giant pasta shells	72

It's simple and convenient to cook pasta dishes in your slow cooker, especially when you're busy and don't have much time. From Spag bol to Lasagne and even Creamy butternut squash pasta, all the dishes in this chapter take no time to prepare, then just let your slow cooker do its thing until you are ready to eat.

Pork and apple orzotto

A throw-it-all-in kinda dish that makes your home smell delicious while you wait for dinnertime! Serve either on its own or with some veg on the side, such as sugar snap peas or a fresh salad works well too.

 Serves 3 adults and 2 littles

 Prep 10 minutes, Cook 3-6 hours

Ingredients

650g (1lb 7oz) pork shoulder steaks, fat trimmed, cut into 2cm (¾in) wide strips

a drizzle of oil

1 brown onion, finely diced

1 low-salt chicken stock cube*

1 bay leaf

2 tsp Dijon mustard (optional)

2 large garlic cloves, minced

1 heaped tsp dried mixed herbs

200g (7oz) orzo pasta*

2 large red eating apples, cored and cut into wedges

freshly ground black pepper

Put half of the pork and a drizzle of oil in a large frying pan over a high heat and cook until browned all over (see p12). This is what will give the final dish its colour and extra depth of flavour, so take a moment to allow it to get some lovely dark charred edges before transferring to your slow cooker pot. Repeat to brown the other half of the meat.

If your pan is dry, add a touch more oil, then turn the heat down and sauté the onion for 3–5 minutes until translucent. Allow the onion to soak up the flavours from the pork cooking juices in the bottom of the pan. Dissolve the stock cube in 400ml (1⅔ cups) water, add to the onions, and stir, then transfer it to the slow cooker pot with the pork. Add a little black pepper, the bay leaf, Dijon mustard, garlic, and the mixed dried herbs to the slow cooker and stir. Put the lid on and cook for 2½ hours on HIGH or 4–5 hours on LOW.

After this time, the pork should be soft and break down with a little pressure. If there is lots of fat sitting at the top of the slow cooker pot, you can skim away a little if you wish using a large spoon. Now add the orzo pasta, apple wedges, and 275ml (scant 1¼ cups) boiling water. Stir and cook on LOW for 30–40 minutes, or until the pasta is cooked through. Add a touch more water if you feel the dish is too dry.

If feeding little ones under 9 months, mash the pork into the orzo using the back of a fork. The apples can be enjoyed as finger food, or also mashed into the dish too.

 Love your leftovers

The orzotto will keep in an airtight container in the fridge for 2–3 days or frozen for 3 months. Reheat with an extra splash of water until piping hot throughout.

Meatballs in tomato sauce

With the surprising addition of pasta in these meatballs, you're left with really tender meat, which isn't overly bready.

Serves 2 adults and 2 littles

Prep 10 minutes, Cook 2-6 hours

Ingredients

2 brown onions, peeled

4 large garlic cloves

1 medium courgette (zucchini)

1kg (2lb 4oz) tomato passata (strained tomatoes)

1 tbsp tomato purée (paste)

50g (1¾oz) Parmesan cheese*, finely grated

4 tsp smoked paprika

1 tbsp Worcestershire sauce (optional)

1 bay leaf

1 tsp dried oregano

1 tsp caster sugar (optional)

2 low-salt beef stock cubes*

500g (1lb 2oz) minced (ground) beef (12% fat)

4 tbsp orzo pasta* (or breadcrumbs*)

1 tsp dried mixed herbs

1 medium egg*

50g (1¾oz) Cheddar cheese*, finely grated

freshly ground black pepper

Gather a large mixing bowl for the meatballs and set up the slow cooker on your worktop with the lid off.

Using a box grater, coarsely grate the onions. Take half of the grated onions in your hands and gently squeeze some of the juice into the remaining onions. Put the drier onion pulp into the bowl and tip the wet onion pulp into the slow cooker pot.

Now, using the fine side of the grater, mince the garlic cloves, adding half to the meatball bowl and half to the slow cooker.

Back to the coarse side of the grater, grate the courgette. Gather a little of the pulp in your hands at a time, hover over the slow cooker and squeeze so that the juices fall into the slow cooker pot, then put the dry courgette pulp into the meatball bowl.

Tip
You can either use all minced (ground) beef that's 12% fat in the meatballs or you can add 250g (9oz) each of minced beef (5% fat) and minced pork (5% fat).

Add the passata, tomato purée, 20g (¾oz) of the Parmesan, 3 teaspoons of the smoked paprika, the Worcestershire sauce, bay leaf, dried oregano, sugar, if using, and a grinding of black pepper to the slow cooker pot. Crumble in the stock cubes, ensuring there are no large lumps. Give it all a very good stir and get on with the meatballs.

Add the mince, orzo pasta, mixed herbs, remaining 1 teaspoon of smoked paprika, egg, a little black pepper, the remaining Parmesan, and all the grated Cheddar to the bowl. Now it's time to get your hands in there – it helps to mix it all up more quickly and evenly.

Once the mixture is well combined, roll it into golf ball-sized meatballs and place each one in the tomato sauce in the slow cooker. You should get around 16 meatballs. Put the lid on and cook for 5–6 hours on LOW, or for 2–3 hours on HIGH.

Serve the meatballs and sauce with pasta, cutting the meatballs in half for little ones.

 Love your leftovers

This will keep for 2 days in the fridge, or will freeze for 3 months. Reheat in a saucepan or in the microwave until each meatball is piping hot throughout.

Chicken Kyiv pasta

This pasta is inspired by the 1970s classic, bringing all the flavours of a chicken Kyiv to a delicious one-pot meal. It's so easy to prepare – add all the ingredients straight into the slow cooker pot in the morning and then it will be ready by dinnertime.

 Serves 2 adults and 2 littles

 Prep 5 minutes, Cook 4-7 hours

Ingredients

600g (1lb 5oz) boneless, skinless chicken thighs

1 large courgette (zucchini), finely grated

3 garlic cloves, puréed or grated

25g (1½ tbsp) unsalted butter*

1 low-salt chicken stock cube*

150g (¾ cup) cream cheese*

150ml (⅔ cup) milk*

250g (9oz) pasta*

50g (1¾oz) grated Cheddar* (optional)

freshly ground black pepper

Add the chicken thighs, grated courgette, garlic, a good grinding of black pepper, and the butter to the slow cooker pot.

Boil the kettle and dissolve the stock cube in 550ml (2½ cups) of water, then add this to the chicken too. Stir really well, so the chicken has unravelled and is submerged under the stock. Pop the lid on and cook on HIGH for 3 hours, or LOW for 6 hours.

Once the chicken is soft and tender, in a separate bowl, add the cream cheese and milk and stir until well combined. Pour this into the slow cooker, along with the uncooked pasta. Stir really well, slightly squashing each piece of chicken with the wooden spoon to help it break up a little.

Put the lid back on and cook for 40 minutes on HIGH or for 1 hour on LOW. Once done, stir really well and then put the lid on to stand for 5 minutes before stirring again and serving.

For an even creamier cheesier texture, add the grated Cheddar once everything is cooked before leaving to stand for 5 minutes. Once done it will have melted into the sauce for a delicious extra flavour.

 Love your leftovers

If you have any left, pour into an ovenproof dish and store in the fridge for 2 days or the freezer for 1 month. Defrost thoroughly, then add a splash more milk to the base of the dish, top with grated cheese, and bake at 200°C fan (220°C/425°F/Gas 7) for 15–20 minutes until golden and crisp on top and piping hot throughout.

Butter chicken pasta

This is a bit of a cuisine mash-up, but my goodness it is delicious! Use your favourite short pasta shape – I prefer using orzo, as it looks like rice in this dish – and serve with some freshly cooked peas and mixed greens.

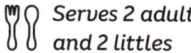
Serves 2 adults and 2 littles

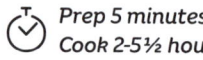
Prep 5 minutes, Cook 2-5½ hours

Ingredients

200ml (scant 1 cup) Greek yogurt*

2 tsp crushed garlic

1½ tsp ground cumin

4 tsp smoked paprika

2 tsp mild garam masala

1 large onion

500g (1lb 2oz) boneless, skinless chicken thighs or breast, cut into large chunks

1 low-salt chicken stock cube*

2 tbsp tomato purée (paste) (optional)

200g (7oz) pasta*

freshly ground black pepper

Add the yogurt, garlic, cumin, paprika, garam masala, and a generous grinding of black pepper to the slow cooker pot. Stir very well, then add the onion either finely diced with a knife or I like to grate mine on a box grater for minimal "onion bits". Add the chicken to the pot too.

Finally, dissolve the stock cube in 400ml (1⅔ cups) of water and the tomato purée, stirring very well, then add this to the slow cooker too, giving everything one final stir to combine. Pop the lid on and cook for 2½ hours on HIGH or 4–5 hours on LOW.

Once done, the chicken should be very tender, give it a stir, then add the pasta and mix in to coat all the pasta pieces in the sauce. Pop the lid back on and cook for a further 25–30 minutes on HIGH until the pasta is cooked through.

Serve with a side of greens with the chicken cut into strips or shredded for little ones. Adults you may want to add some salt to your portion too.

 Love your leftovers

Leftovers will store in an airtight container in the fridge for 3 days or freeze for up to 3 months. Allow to thaw in the fridge, then reheat in a saucepan until piping hot throughout; you may need to add a splash of water to help loosen the sauce.

Tip
For the chicken, I like to use thigh meat as it's the juiciest, but breast will also work.

Tip
You can use either all minced (ground) beef that's 10–15% fat or equal quantities of minced beef and minced pork.

Traditional Bolognese

 GF*

 EF

DF*

There's something about a Bolognese sauce that has had time to cook for hours – the flavours have developed, the veg is soft, and the whole meal is as comforting as you remember from your childhood.

 Serves 6

 Prep 20 minutes, Cook 3-8 hours

Ingredients

750g–1kg (1lb 10oz–2lb 4oz) minced (ground) beef (10–15% fat)

3 rashers of smoked bacon, thinly sliced (optional)

3 medium carrots, peeled (if you like) and diced

3 celery sticks, finely diced

1 large onion, finely diced

a drizzle of garlic-infused olive oil (optional)

3 fat garlic cloves, minced

2 tbsp tomato purée (paste)

1 heaped tsp mixed herbs

1 tbsp Worcestershire sauce (optional)

1 heaped tsp sugar

1 tbsp smoked paprika

2 low-salt beef stock cubes*

500g (1lb 2oz) tomato passata (strained tomatoes)

1 x 400g (14oz) can of chopped tomatoes

freshly ground black pepper

Put the mince and bacon, if using, in a large dry frying pan and cook until the mince has browned and is taking on a darker colour – this will take around 5–7 minutes (see p.12). Transfer the meat to your slow cooker pot. At this stage you can scrunch up a few pieces of kitchen paper and dab into the meat to remove some of the excess fat, if you wish.

Meanwhile, in the same frying pan in which you cooked the meat, fry the carrots, celery, and onion in the remaining meat juices. Add a touch of garlic-infused oil if you feel like your pan is very dry. Sauté the veggies for around 5 minutes until soft (see p.12), then transfer to the slow cooker.

While everything is frying, add the garlic, tomato purée, mixed herbs, Worcestershire sauce, sugar, and paprika to the slow cooker, along with a good grind of black pepper, then crumble in the beef stock cubes. Now, add the tomato passata, and half fill the carton with water from the tap, swilling it around to loosen any of the excess tomato hiding in the packet, and add to the slow cooker. Add the can of chopped tomatoes and do the same, quarter-filling the can and swilling around before adding the liquid to the slow cooker.

Once everything has been added to the slow cooker, give it a very good stir, then pop the lid on and cook for 6–8 hours on LOW or for 3–4 hours on HIGH.

Once ready, serve the sauce with a pasta shape of your choice and with a little grated cheese on top. Adults, you can season your portion on your plate if you feel it needs it.

 Love your leftovers

The sauce will keep for up to 4 days in an airtight container in the fridge, or freeze for up to 3 months. Defrost and reheat on the hob or in the microwave until piping hot throughout.

Spag bol mac and cheese

This recipe combines spaghetti Bolognese and macaroni cheese into one gorgeous meal that's creamy, cheesy, and comforting – need I say more?!

 Serves 3 adults and 3 littles

 Prep 10 minutes, Cook 2½–4½ hours

Ingredients

500g (1lb 2oz) lean minced (ground) beef

2 large carrots

500g (1lb 2oz) passata (strained tomatoes)

2 tbsp tomato purée (paste)

650ml (2¾ cups) milk*

1 tsp dried porcini mushroom powder (optional)

1 low-salt beef stock cube*, crumbled

1 tsp Dijon mustard (optional)

1 tsp garlic granules

2 tsp smoked paprika

2 tsp dried mixed herbs

350g (3⅓ cups) dried macaroni pasta*

150g (5½oz) Cheddar cheese*, grated

100g (½ cup) cream cheese*

freshly ground black pepper

Set a large non-stick frying pan over a high heat to warm up. When the pan is hot, add the beef and break it up using a wooden spoon. Cook for 4–5 minutes until browned. Try to avoid touching the meat too much as it cooks so that it has lots of contact with the hot pan and gains some caramelized bits, as this is where the flavour is (see p.12).

Meanwhile, wash, then finely dice or coarsely grate the carrots – no need to peel them as there's lots of goodness in the skin. Add the carrots to the slow cooker pot along with the passata, tomato purée, half of the milk, the mushroom powder, if using, crumbled stock cube, Dijon mustard, garlic granules, paprika, mixed herbs, and plenty of black pepper.

Add the beef once it's browned and stir well. Pop the lid on the slow cooker and cook for 2 hours on HIGH or for 4 hours on LOW.

Now remove the lid, add the rest of the milk and the macaroni pasta. Stir really well, cover, and cook for a further 20–40 minutes on LOW, or until the pasta is cooked. The time really depends on your pasta and your slow cooker – it should soften quickly and easily, so taste to check the texture after 20 minutes and if it's not done, give it another 10 minutes, then check again. Once the pasta is soft, add the Cheddar cheese and cream cheese, stir, and allow to stand for a few moments before serving.

 Love your leftovers

Transfer leftovers to an ovenproof dish immediately to stop the cooking process, and prepare for turning them into a pasta bake. Keep in the fridge for up to 2 days. Reheat in the oven at 200°C fan (220°C/425°F/Gas 7), with a little extra cheese on top, and bake until piping hot. You can also freeze leftovers for up to 2 months. Defrost thoroughly and then reheat as above or in the microwave for 2–3 minutes on HIGH.

Hodgepodge shortcut lasagne

Italian traditionalists, please look away now! This throw-it-together dish tastes like an oven-baked layered lasagne, but the cooking method is a lot simpler. It looks a little scruffier, but saves you time cutting everything up for the little ones.

 Serves 3 adults and 2 littles

 Prep 10 minutes, Cook 2-3 hours

Ingredients

1 tbsp garlic-infused oil

500g (1lb 2oz) minced (ground) beef (5–10% fat)

500g (1lb 2oz) passata (strained tomatoes)

2 x 400g (14oz) cans of chopped tomatoes

3 tsp garlic purée

2 tsp dried mixed herbs

2 heaped tsp smoked paprika

250g (1 cup) ricotta cheese*

250g (1 cup) mascarpone cheese*

50ml (¼ cup) milk*

2 tbsp tomato purée (paste)

300g (10½oz) fresh lasagne sheets*

80g (2¾oz) Cheddar cheese*, grated

freshly ground black pepper

Heat a large, non-stick frying pan over the highest heat on the hob. Add the garlic oil to the pan, followed by the beef. Use a wooden spoon to break up the meat, then leave it alone for 2 minutes to cook (see p.12).

Meanwhile, add the passata and cans of chopped tomatoes to the slow cooker pot, along with 2 teaspoons of the garlic purée, the dried herbs, smoked paprika, and black pepper to taste.

Give the mince a stir, breaking up any lumps and cook for a further 2 minutes.

Meanwhile, add the ricotta, mascarpone, the remaining teaspoon of garlic purée, and the milk to a medium bowl. Stir together well, then set aside.

Add the tomato purée to the browned mince and cook, stirring, for 1 minute. Tip the meat into the slow cooker pot and stir thoroughly.

For all but one of the lasagne sheets, scrumple them up in your hands to break them into small pieces, then add to the slow cooker. Stir well to submerge the pasta in the sauce, ensuring it's evenly spread around the whole pot. Lay the remaining whole lasagne sheet on top of everything in the middle, then spread over the cheese sauce, reaching right to the edges. Sprinkle the grated cheese on top. Lay several sheets of kitchen paper over the top of the slow cooker pot to soak up excess moisture and pop the lid on. Pull the paper so it is taught under the lid and not flopping down into the food. Cook for 2–3 hours on LOW, or until the pasta is soft. If you want a crispy top, you can brown the lasagne (minus the kitchen paper) under the grill, if your slow cooker pot allows it.

Allow to stand for 10 minutes before serving alongside a refreshing side salad.

 Love your leftovers

This dish is best served fresh; however, leftovers will keep for 2 days in the fridge. They can be reheated in a hot oven for around 20 minutes with an extra splash of water. You can also freeze leftovers for up to 2 months. Reheat from frozen for 35 minutes until piping hot throughout.

Tingle those taste buds
To ramp up the flavour, when frying the mince, crumble a low-salt beef stock cube into the pan and add a teaspoon of sugar to the tomato sauce.

Creamy butternut squash pasta

A veg-packed meal that is so simple to throw together. Even the fussiest eaters will love it.

Serves 2 hungry adults and 3 littles

Prep 10 minutes, Cook 3½–6½ hours

Ingredients

1 large butternut squash, peeled, deseeded, and roughly chopped (approx. 800g–1kg/1lb 12oz–2lb 4oz chopped weight)

1 onion, roughly chopped

3 large garlic cloves, roughly chopped

1 low-salt chicken or vegetable stock cube*

220g (7¾oz) dried pasta of your choice*

200ml (scant 1 cup) milk*

100g (½ cup) cream cheese*

90g (3¼oz) smoked Cheddar cheese*, grated

2 tsp smoked paprika

freshly ground black pepper

Boil the kettle.

Add the chopped butternut squash, onion, and garlic to your slow cooker pot along with a generous grinding of black pepper. Crumble in the stock cube, then add 500ml (generous 2 cups) of boiling water from the kettle. Stir to dissolve the stock cube, then pop the lid on and cook for 3 hours on HIGH or for 5–6 hours on LOW until the veg is very tender.

Once it's ready, blend the veg and cooking liquid to a very smooth purée, either with a stick blender or decant into a food processor, then pour back into the slow cooker. The mixture you have is now essentially butternut squash soup, which you can always thin down to your desired consistency and serve as it is, if you'd like.

Today we're making pasta, so add the uncooked pasta, the milk, cream cheese, grated smoked cheese, and smoked paprika to the butternut squash purée and stir well. Place the lid back on the slow cooker and cook for a further 30–40 minutes on LOW, or until the pasta is cooked.

Serve this up as it is. Adults, feel free to add a touch of salt and pepper to your portions.

This dish is also fantastic the next day as a pasta bake. Simply pour into an oven dish with a splash more milk, top with extra grated cheese, and bake at 200°C fan (220°C/425°F/Gas 7) for around 20 minutes, or until the cheese is crisp and golden on top.

♡ Love your leftovers

Leftovers will keep for up to 2 days in the fridge, or freeze for up to 3 months. The pasta will keep cooking in the hot slow cooker, so decant leftovers into a bowl to stop the cooking process. It will also thicken once cool, so add a splash of milk when reheating. To reheat, either cook until piping hot in a pan, or pop in the microwave for 2–3 minutes on HIGH. If frozen, defrost thoroughly and reheat as above.

Ricotta and tuna stuffed giant pasta shells

Soft and creamy tuna filling, stuffed into comically giant pasta shells, on a bed of rich tomato and pea sauce. The shells are perfectly shaped for little fingers to handle.

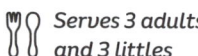

Serves 3 adults and 3 littles

Prep 20 minutes, Cook 2-3 hours

Ingredients

1 tbsp cornflour (cornstarch)

500g (1lb 2oz) passata (strained tomatoes)

1 tsp dried mixed herbs

2 heaped tsp smoked paprika

2 tsp garlic granules

1 tbsp Worcestershire sauce (optional)

1 tsp sugar (optional)

1 low-salt chicken or vegetable stock cube*

200g (7oz) dried conchiglioni* (giant pasta shells – can substitute cannelloni tubes)

2 x 110g (3¾oz) cans tuna in spring water, drained

250g (generous 1 cup) ricotta cheese* (or thick dairy-free cream cheese)

70g (2½oz) Cheddar cheese*, grated

250g (9oz) frozen peas

freshly ground black pepper

In a small bowl, mix the cornflour with 1 tablespoon of water until you have a smooth, runny paste.

Pour the passata, herbs, paprika, half of the garlic granules, the cornflour paste, Worcestershire sauce, and sugar, if using, into the slow cooker pot and stir to combine. Boil the kettle. Crumble your stock cube into the passata container and fill with 200ml (scant 1 cup) of hot water. Pour the stock into the slow cooker, stir again, pop the lid on, and cook on HIGH for 30 minutes.

Meanwhile, place the pasta shells in a large, heatproof bowl big enough to cover the shells with water. Pour more boiling water over the pasta and leave for 1 minute before draining. Cool slightly.

In a small bowl, mix the tuna, ricotta, 30g (1oz) of the Cheddar, a little black pepper, and the remaining 1 teaspoon of garlic granules. Hold a pasta shell in the cup of your hand, holding it open slightly. Take a generous ½ tablespoon of the tuna mixture, point the spoon inside the pasta shell, and use your thumb to scrape the filling inside the pasta. Place the shell on a large plate or tray and repeat until you have used up all of the filling.

Lift the lid, stir the sauce, and add the peas, then carefully place the pasta shells snugly next to each other on top of the sauce, open side up. Pop the lid on again and cook on LOW for 1½ hours.

Remove the lid and sprinkle the shells with the remaining cheese and a little black pepper. Cook on HIGH for 30–40 minutes until the peas are cooked through and the cheese is bubbling at the sides. Serve in bowls with extra boiled veg, if you like. You can serve the stuffed shells whole to little ones, or slice in half lengthways.

 Love your leftovers

Leftovers will keep for 2 days in the fridge. Reheat in the oven for around 15 minutes until piping hot.

Tip
If your kiddos prefer their veg mixed in with their meal, rather than on the side, add a small grated and squeezed courgette (zucchini) to the tuna mixture. Alternatively, wilt some spinach and squeeze out the excess moisture, then chop and add that to the tuna mixture.

Easy Weeknight

Chickpea and butternut squash dahl	78
Turkey chilli	81
Mushroom ragù	82
Broccoli slice	84
Cajun pork and mash	87
Coconut potato curry	88
Courgette and tomato risotto	90
Nina's favourite tender lemon garlic chicken	93
Mushroom risotto	94
Sweet potato and chickpea curry	97
Comforting chicken soup with bread dumplings	98
Peanut butter chicken curry	101

Incredibly easy to put together, just throw all your ingredients into your slow cooker pot and allow your dish to simmer away while you get on with your day. All these recipes are very simple to rustle up for a perfect midweek meal when you are busy with work and your family.
It's a win-win.

Chickpea and butternut squash dahl

A hearty vegan meal, creamy in texture and full of protein and goodness from the lentils and chickpeas, making it well balanced and nutritious for all the family. Serve the dahl with rice or naan breads, or you could even serve it as a pasta sauce.

 Serves 2 adults and 3 littles

 Prep 5 mins, Cook 3–8 hours

Ingredients

1 butternut squash, peeled and cut into 2cm (¾in) dice

1 x 400g (14oz) can of chickpeas in water

300g (1⅔ cups) dried red lentils, rinsed

2 low-salt vegetable stock cubes*

1 tbsp garam masala

1 tbsp mild curry powder

a good grinding of black pepper

2 heaped tsp dried mixed herbs

2 tsp smoked paprika

1 x 400g (14oz) can of coconut milk

1 x 400g (14oz) can of chopped tomatoes

1 brown onion, finely diced

2 garlic cloves, grated

Put all of the ingredients, including the water from the can of chickpeas, into the slow cooker pot, along with 350ml (1½ cups) of boiling water. Give it a really good stir and pop the lid on. Cook for 3–4 hours on HIGH or for 6–8 hours on LOW. Once done, use a wooden spoon or rubber spatula to give the dahl a really good stir and mash the soft butternut squash into the sauce a little.

Serve. Adults, you may want to season your portion with a little salt or even a dash of chilli sauce, if you like.

 Love your leftovers

The dahl will keep for 3 days in the fridge, or freeze for 3 months. Reheat in a saucepan or in the microwave until bubbling and piping hot throughout.

Tip
If serving to under 2s, mash or blitz the kidney beans before adding to the pan, as large beans can pose a choking hazard for little eaters.

Turkey chilli

Turkey mince is often cheaper than beef mince when comparing the same quality. It is also lower in saturated fat, making this chilli a much healthier version.

Serves 2 adults and 2 littles

Prep 8 minutes, Cook 3-8 hours

Ingredients

1 medium onion (optional)

1 tbsp sunflower oil

500g (1lb 2oz) minced (ground) turkey or chicken (or plant-based mince)*

2 tsp ground cumin

2 tsp garlic granules

3 tsp smoked paprika

1 low-salt chicken or beef stock cube*

1 tsp dried mixed herbs

280g (9½oz) frozen sweetcorn or unsalted canned

1 x 400g (14oz) can of kidney beans in water (salt free)

1 x 400g (14oz) can of chopped tomatoes

freshly ground black pepper

If using, grate the onion on the coarse side of a box grater.

Heat the oil in a frying pan, add the onion, and sauté for approx. 3 minutes, stirring often until it starts to turn translucent (see p12). Now add the mince, and begin to break it up with a wooden spoon, stirring well. Cook for a further 3 minutes, continuing to break up the meat into smaller chunks as it cooks (see p12)

Add the mince to the slow cooker pot with the rest of the ingredients. Stir really well, pop the lid on, and cook for 3 hours on HIGH or for 6–8 hours on LOW.

Serve with rice and avocado if you have it, or a simple salad also works amazingly. Don't forget the grated cheese to melt on the hot chilli on your plate – the best bit!

Love your leftovers

This chilli will last for 2 days in an airtight container in the fridge, or freeze for up to 3 months. Thaw thoroughly before reheating in a saucepan until bubbling and piping hot throughout.

Mushroom ragù

GF* EF DF* V Vg*

A meat-free dinner option with deep, rich umami flavours that are intensified through slow cooking. Because the mushrooms have been grated and slowly cooked, they melt into the sauce, making it perfect for little taste testers.

Serves 2 adults and 3 littles

Prep 8 minutes, Cook 3½–6 hours

Ingredients

2 low-salt vegetable or chicken stock cubes*

500g (1lb 2oz) chestnut mushrooms, wiped clean

1 large brown onion

500g (1lb 2oz) passata (strained tomatoes)

2 tbsp tomato purée (paste)

2 tsp dried mixed herbs

2 tbsp Worcestershire sauce (optional)

10–15g (¼–½oz) dried porcini mushrooms

2 tsp dried porcini mushroom powder (optional)

a little freshly ground black pepper

Fill the kettle with water and put it on to boil.

Crumble the stock cubes into a jug, then pour over 400ml (1⅔ cups) of boiling water from the kettle, stirring to dissolve.

Coarsely grate the mushrooms and onion using a box grater or the grater attachment in a food processor, which will be much quicker.

Add the grated vegetable pulp to the slow cooker pot along with the stock and the rest of the ingredients. If your dried mushroom pieces are very large, use kitchen scissors or a sharp knife to chop them down to 1cm (½in) pieces before adding.

Pop the lid on the slow cooker and cook for 3½ hours on HIGH or 5–6 hours on LOW (it can actually bubble away on LOW for a bit longer if needed).

Serve with freshly cooked pasta or on jacket potatoes for a warming and comforting family meal.

 Love your leftovers

Leftovers will keep for up to 3 days in the fridge. Reheat in a saucepan or in the microwave for 2–3 minutes on HIGH until piping hot. This dish can also be frozen for up to 4 months. Defrost, then reheat as above.

Broccoli slice

This slice is like a crustless cheesy broccoli quiche, delicious and simple with a salad and some bread, or in a burger bun with some sliced cucumber and relish. Prep in the morning and that's lunch sorted for later.

 Serves 3 adults and 2 littles

 Prep 5 minutes, Cook 1½–3 hours

Ingredients

1 head of broccoli

125g (½ cup) cream cheese*

8 medium eggs

85g (3oz) Cheddar cheese*, grated

1 tsp garlic powder

1 tsp onion powder

Cut a piece of non-stick baking paper to slightly larger than the circumference of your slow cooker pot. Crumple it up into a small ball, then unravel it so it's flat again, which will make it more pliable. Press the paper into the base of your slow cooker pot.

Wash the broccoli and cut into very small florets. If you wish, you can remove as much of the stalk as possible and finely chop that too. Add the broccoli to the slow cooker on top of the baking paper.

Add the cream cheese and 4 of the eggs to a mixing bowl. Using a balloon whisk, mix the cream cheese into the egg until you can see no lumps, then add the remaining eggs, grated cheese, and garlic and onion powders. Whisk well to combine. Pour the egg mixture on top of the broccoli and give it a little poke to ensure the broccoli is sitting mostly under the liquid and distributed evenly.

Take 4 squares of kitchen paper, still attached in a long line, and fold over in half. Place over the lip of the slow cooker pot, and if it doesn't reach all the way round, repeat with another double layer of kitchen paper. Pop the lid on the slow cooker, and gently tease the paper so it is tight and doesn't droop down into the food. This will soak up any excess moisture, so that the slice doesn't become too soggy.

Cook for about 1½ hours on HIGH, or 2–3 hours on LOW, until the egg mixture feels firm and the broccoli has softened. Remove from the slow cooker, using the baking paper to lift it up, and cut into 8 sections, or into finger strips if serving to little ones under 2 years.

 Love your leftovers

The slice will keep in the fridge for 2 days, or freeze for 2 months. Reheat in the oven or microwave until piping hot throughout.

Tips
You can swap the broccoli for other veg you have in your fridge, like grated courgette (zucchini) or carrot. If you would like to bulk the dish out, add some chopped ham, cooked potatoes, or chunks of bread, which will soak up some of the egg.

Tip
For little ones, cut the pork into finger strips and serve the mash on a preloaded spoon. Adults, add a little salt to your portion if you wish.

Cajun pork and mash

Cook your meat and potatoes in one pot so that those meat juices and spices flavour the mash deliciously. Plus, there's some hidden veggies in those spuds too: win-win!

 **Serves 2 adults and 2 littles**

 **Prep 10 minutes, Cook 2½–6 hours**

Ingredients

sunflower oil, for cooking

4 pork shoulder steaks

800g (1lb 12oz) all-rounder potatoes

400g (14oz) swede, peeled and diced

1 low-salt chicken stock cube*, crumbled

1 tsp ground cumin

2 tsp smoked paprika

2 tsp garlic granules

freshly ground black pepper

Heat a large frying pan over a high heat with a little oil. Sear the pork for a minute on each side, working in 2 batches to avoid overcrowding the pan. You want to quickly seal the meat to keep in the juices and flavour, but not cook it all the way through (see p12). Then transfer to a plate and set aside.

Peel and cube the potatoes into approx. 2cm (¾in) chunks, then cut the swede a little smaller. Add to your slow cooker pot along with the crumbled stock cube.

In a small bowl, add the cumin, paprika, garlic granules, and a good grinding of black pepper and stir to combine. Add half of this mixture to the potatoes and swede and stir to combine. Then measure 400ml (1⅔ cups) of water in a jug and add to the frying pan you seared the pork steaks in, with the heat off. Briefly stir to dissolve any cooking juices into the liquid, then pour this over the potatoes. Stir very well and even out the potatoes and swede.

With the remaining spice mix, sprinkle half over the top of the pork steaks, then place these spiced-side down in the slow cooker on the potatoes, avoiding overlapping the meat. They won't be submerged in the liquid, but that's fine. Sprinkle over the remaining spice mix and pop the lid on.

Cook for 3½ hours on HIGH or for 6 hours on LOW. Once done, the meat will be very tender and the potatoes cooked through. Carefully transfer the pork to a serving plate, trying to keep each piece whole, and spoon over a little juice on each one to keep it moist and warm. Now, using a potato masher, mash the spuds and swede to a smooth purée before serving up alongside the pork.

 Love your leftovers

Leftovers will keep for 2 days in the fridge. Reheat the pork at 180°C fan (200°C/400°F/Gas 6) in an ovenproof dish with a little dash of water, covered with foil, for 15–20 minutes until piping hot throughout. The mash can be microwaved for 3 minutes, or reheated in a saucepan with a little more water too. You can also freeze this dish for up to 1 month, defrosting thoroughly and reheating as above.

Easy Weeknight

Coconut potato curry

The humble potato is the star of the show in this delicious curry. Serve as a main dish or a side with flatbread or freshly cooked rice.

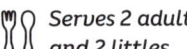 **Serves 2 adults and 2 littles**

 Prep 10 minutes, Cook 3½–6 hours

Ingredients

1 large onion

2 large garlic cloves

2 tbsp garlic-infused olive oil

2 tbsp tomato purée (paste)

2 tsp garam masala

1 heaped tbsp mild curry powder

1 x 400g (14oz) can of coconut milk

1 low-salt vegetable stock cube*

1kg (2lb 4oz) all-rounder potatoes, like Maris piper

4 lumps of frozen spinach (about 200g/7oz)

3–4 flatbreads*, to serve

Peel and grate the onion on a box grater, or finely dice. Finely grate the garlic, then add the onion and garlic with the oil to the slow cooker pot and stir. Pop the lid on and cook for 10–15 minutes on HIGH.

Meanwhile, peel the potatoes and dice into bite-sized chunks (about 3cm/1¼in). Set aside.

Add the tomato purée, garam masala, and curry powder to the slow cooker pot and stir. Put the lid back on and cook for a further 10 minutes. Fill the kettle with water and put it on to boil.

Once everything is smelling aromatic in the slow cooker and the onion has started to cook, add the coconut milk and potatoes. Carefully fill the coconut milk can with boiling water, crumble in the stock cube, and add to the slow cooker. Stir, pop back the lid on, and cook for 3 hours on HIGH or for 5 hours on LOW.

After this time, add the frozen spinach to the slow cooker, put the lid back on, and cook for a further 30 minutes on HIGH or 1 hour on LOW.

To serve, pile the curry into bowls and tuck a flatbread into the side of each dish. Adults, feel free to add a little salt to your curry, and for babies, mash any pieces of potato, which are too small for baby to hold.

 Love your leftovers

The curry will keep for 2 days in the fridge, or freeze for 3 months. Reheat with an extra splash of water in a saucepan or microwave. The flatbreads can be stored for 3 days in an airtight container, or frozen for 3 months. Reheat in the microwave for 90–120 seconds, or on a baking tray in the oven with a little splash of water for 5–10 minutes.

Courgette and tomato risotto

With this risotto you simply throw it all into the slow cooker pot and give it a good stir right at the end. Risotto has never been so easy! Serve with a simple side salad or some crusty bread for a more substantial meal.

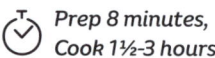

Serves 3 adults and 2 littles

Prep 8 minutes, Cook 1½–3 hours

Ingredients

2 low-salt chicken or vegetable stock cubes*

oil or butter, for greasing

1 large courgette (zucchini)

1 onion

300g (1½ cups) risotto rice

1 tsp garlic granules

1 x 400g (14oz) can of good-quality cherry tomatoes

2 tbsp unsalted butter*

80g (2¾oz) Cheddar cheese*, grated

50g (¼ cup) cream cheese*

freshly ground black pepper

Put the kettle on to boil. Crumble the stock cubes into a jug, then fill it with 1 litre (4¼ cups) of boiling water. Stir to dissolve the stock cubes.

Lightly grease the inside of the slow cooker pot with oil or butter to avoid the rice sticking. Coarsely grate the courgette and onion on a box grater or using the grater attachment on a food processor. Add the grated veg to the slow cooker along with the stock, risotto rice, garlic granules, and a little black pepper. Add the can of cherry tomatoes, then quarter-fill the empty can with cold tap water and swill out any remaining tomato juice, adding this to the slow cooker too.

Stir well, pop the lid on and cook for 1½–2½ hours on HIGH. The time really depends on the size and power of your slow cooker. Check after about an hour, then at 30-minute intervals by giving it a good stir and having a taste of the rice when it's starting to look done. If the rice doesn't taste grainy or crunchy and the majority of the water has been absorbed, then it's done. If it needs more cooking, add a touch more boiling water if it's looking dry, and cook for a further 20–30 minutes before checking again.

Once done, add the butter, Cheddar cheese, and cream cheese and stir to melt them into the risotto. They will transform the consistency of the dish to make it super creamy.

Serve with extra seasoning for the adults, if you wish.

 Love your leftovers

Leftovers will keep for up to 24 hours in the fridge or 3 months in the freezer. If you plan to keep some, immediately spread the leftover risotto out onto a cold plate to help it cool quickly so that it's at a safe temperature for storing. Once cool, scoop into an airtight container and chill or freeze straight away. Defrost in the fridge overnight if needed, then reheat in a saucepan with a splash of water until piping hot.

Nina's favourite tender lemon garlic chicken

 GF*
 EF
DF*

When I made this throw-it-all-in-one-pot dish for my three-year-old Nina the "yummy" noises she was making filled me with happiness. "This is so good Mummy, you have to put it in your new book." Well, Nina, it's going in!

 Serves 2 adults and 2 littles

 Prep 10 minutes, Cook 5 hours

Ingredients

500g (1lb 2oz) skinless, boneless chicken thighs

finely grated zest and juice of 1 large unwaxed lemon

2 large garlic cloves, finely grated

2 tsp dried mixed herbs

1 low-salt chicken stock cube*

35g (1¼oz) unsalted butter*, cubed

500g (1lb 2oz) mini new potatoes

freshly ground black pepper

Add the chicken thighs, the lemon zest and juice, the garlic, herbs, and a little black pepper to the slow cooker pot.

Crumble the stock cube into a jug and add the butter. Pour over 175ml (¾ cup) of boiling water from the kettle and allow to dissolve. Pour over the chicken and cook for 3–4 hours on LOW or until the chicken is just starting to fall apart. Add the potatoes and cook for a further 1 hour until they are super tender.

Serve with steamed veg and a little crusty bread to soak up the juices. For little taste testers, slice the potatoes in half lengthways or mash them into the chicken juices, which is delicious for us adults too, by the way!

 Love your leftovers

The dish will keep for 2 days in the fridge, or freeze for 3 months. Defrost thoroughly before reheating until piping hot in the oven or microwave.

Mushroom risotto

Silky mushroom risotto packed full of rich, earthy flavours, this is a family favourite in my house!

Serves 2 adults and 2 littles

Prep 20 minutes, Cook 3-4 hours

Ingredients

15g (½oz) dried porcini mushrooms

1 low-salt chicken or vegetable stock cube*

1 medium onion

35g (2½ tbsp) unsalted butter*

200g (7oz) chestnut mushrooms

2 fat garlic cloves, grated or crushed

150g (¾ cup) arborio risotto rice

a large handful (about 40g/1½oz) hard cheese, such as Cheddar*, grated

freshly ground black pepper

Boil the kettle. Put the dried mushrooms in a jug and crumble in the stock cube. Fill with 650ml (generous 2¾ cups) of boiling water from the kettle, stir, and set aside to let the mushrooms soften.

Meanwhile, peel and finely dice the onion (as small as you can). Add 25g (1oz) of the butter to a medium frying pan and allow it to melt while adding the onion. Sauté for 3 minutes (see p12) while you chop the fresh mushrooms. Finely dice the mushrooms by slicing each into 3 or 4, then chopping roughly into smaller pieces. Add the mushrooms and garlic to the onion, along with a little pepper, and cook for 5 minutes. Transfer to the slow cooker pot on LOW. If you don't want to use a pan for this, you can do this process in a slow cooker and add everything to the slow cooker pot on HIGH for 30 minutes, stirring halfway.

Remove the soaked mushrooms from the broth and put them on a chopping board. Set the broth aside. Run a knife over the mushrooms to cut them into small pieces, as fine as you can. Add these to the slow cooker pot with the rice and cook for 5 minutes, ensuring all the rice is coated with a little bit of butter.

Pour the mushroom stock into the slow cooker, stir once more, then pop the lid on. Cook for 2 hours on LOW, stirring halfway through.

After 2 hours, check to see whether the liquid has been absorbed by the rice. If there is no more liquid remaining, add a splash or 2 of water from the kettle and cook for a further 1 hour. When the rice is cooked (it should still have a little bite and not be mushy!), turn the slow cooker off and add the remaining butter, along with the grated cheese, and stir to melt. The risotto will suddenly become silky and creamy.

For little ones, you can serve as is or blend a little to smooth out any larger lumps for young babies, if you like. Ensure there are no large lumps of mushroom in any portions for under 2s. Adults, you can add a touch more cheese and a little salt to your portion, if you wish.

 Love your leftovers

Rice must be cooled down within the hour for it to be safely stored and reheated. Spread the risotto on a cold plate to cool very quickly, then spoon into a bowl, cover tightly, and refrigerate for up to 2 days. To reheat, put it in a saucepan with an extra splash of water or stock and simmer until piping hot throughout. You can freeze the risotto for up to 3 months – defrost thoroughly in the fridge overnight before reheating, as above, within 24 hours.

Sweet potato and chickpea curry

Incredibly easy to throw together, this is a bung-it-all-in-the-pot kinda recipe. With protein-packed chickpeas and a sweet, creamy, mildly spiced flavour, this veg-packed curry is great for both little ones and adults.

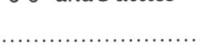

Serves 2 adults and 3 littles

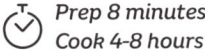

Prep 8 minutes, Cook 4–8 hours

Ingredients

1kg (2lb 4oz) sweet potatoes

1 onion, finely diced or grated

1 x 400g (14oz) can of crushed tomatoes

1 x 400g (14oz) can of coconut milk

1 x 400g (14oz) can of chickpeas in water, drained

1 tbsp mild curry powder

1 tbsp mild garam masala

2 tsp ground turmeric

2 tsp minced fresh garlic or garlic granules

2 tsp finely grated fresh ginger (optional)

6 cubes of frozen spinach

a good grinding of black pepper

Peel the sweet potatoes and roughly chop them into 2.5cm (1in) chunks. Add these to the slow cooker pot along with the rest of the ingredients.

Fill the empty tomato can a quarter of the way with cold tap water, swill it round to catch any tomato residue and add this to the slow cooker pot too. Stir well, pop the lid on, and cook for 4 hours on HIGH or 7–8 hours on LOW until the sweet potatoes are very soft.

If you prefer a less chunky texture, use a potato masher to roughly mash all the potato chunks until you can't see any large lumps, this will instantly thicken the curry. Serve over a bed of rice or with flatbreads for dunking. To help baby pick it up and enjoy their meal independently, you can try serving the rice mixed with curry on a spoon, or form into rough balls by squishing it together in your hands. Adults feel free to add a dash of hot chilli sauce to your portion and a sprinkling of salt, if you desire.

Got an extra minute? To intensify the curry flavour, while you peel the spuds, sauté the onion in a frying pan with a touch of oil until soft and translucent. Add the spices and cook for 30–60 seconds, taking care not to let them burn, before adding the tomatoes. Frying spices like this releases their flavour even more. Add the spiced tomatoes to the slow cooker with the remaining ingredients and cook as above.

♡ Love your leftovers

Leftovers will keep for up to 3 days in the fridge, or freeze for up to 4 months. To reheat from chilled or defrosted, place in a saucepan until bubbling. You can also microwave the curry from frozen for 3–5 minutes on HIGH until piping hot throughout.

Comforting chicken soup with bread dumplings

Feeling under the weather, or just need warming up on a cold, wintery day? This soup will do the trick! You can use chicken thighs or leftover meat from a roast chicken.

 Serves 2 adults and 2 littles

 **Prep 30 minutes, Cook 3½-4 hours**

Ingredients

1 low-salt chicken stock cube*

4 chicken thighs

1 tbsp olive oil

2 large carrots, peeled

2 celery sticks

1 bay leaf (optional)

1 tsp dried mixed herbs

For the dumplings

6 slices of white bread*

2 medium eggs

½ tsp dried mixed herbs

freshly ground black pepper

Put the kettle on to boil. Crumble the stock cube into a jug, then fill it with 1 litre (4¼ cups) of boiling water. Stir to dissolve the stock cubes.

Remove the skin from the chicken but leave the bone in – this will give flavour to the soup. Put the chicken in a large saucepan with the oil and cook over a medium-high heat for 4–5 minutes until browned and partially cooked. Set aside. Skip this step if using leftover meat from a roast chicken.

Roughly slice the carrots and celery on the diagonal into large 4cm (1½in) chunks. Chopping into larger chunks makes it easier to remove when serving, if little ones prefer not to eat these. Add the veg and chicken to the slow cooker pot, then pour over the stock, and add the bay leaf, if using, and mixed herbs. Pop the lid on and cook for 3 hours on LOW.

Meanwhile, make the dumplings. If the crusts on your slices of bread are tough, remove them; however, if they are soft, it's fine to keep them on. Slice the bread into 1cm (½in) cubes, or as small as you can. Alternatively, you can whizz up the bread in a food processor.

Put the bread in a mixing bowl, along with the eggs, herbs, and a little black pepper. Give it a really good stir and get your hands in to squish the bread into the egg to help it soak up as much as possible. Allow to stand for a minute before rolling the mixture into 8–10 golf ball-sized balls. You may need to cup the mixture in the palms of your hands to squeeze it together into balls, but once you get the dumplings in the pan, they will hold together. Chill until your soup has been cooking for 3 hours.

At this point, remove the chicken thighs, if using, then pull the meat from the chicken bones and add it back to the soup. Gently place the bread dumplings in the soup and cook for a further 30 minutes until the dumplings are hot and feel firm to the touch. Serve in bowls, together or deconstructed for little taste testers. You can serve the broth in a cup if you wish, and the dumplings in halves or quarters. Adults, feel free to add salt to your portion.

 Love your leftovers

If you've used fresh chicken, the soup will keep for 2 days in the fridge, or freeze for 2 months. Defrost and reheat in a saucepan until piping hot throughout.

Tip
Use the leftover bones from your Sunday roast chicken instead of thighs here, to make your meals stretch even further.

Peanut butter chicken curry

A creamy, rich and nutty sauce coating succulent pieces of chicken. You can swap the meat for butternut squash or chunks of tofu to make this dish meat free.

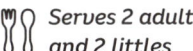

Serves 2 adults and 2 littles

Prep 15 minutes, Cook 3-6 hours

Ingredients

500–600g (1lb 2oz–1lb 5oz) skinless, boneless chicken thighs, cut into 1cm (½in) wide strips

2 tsp mild curry powder

2 tsp smoked paprika

2 tsp garlic-infused or sunflower oil (optional)

1 medium white onion

3 small garlic cloves

15g (1 tbsp) unsalted butter*

4 tbsp 100% nut peanut butter (smooth or crunchy)

2 tbsp low-salt light soy sauce*

1 low-salt chicken stock cube*

1 x 400g (14oz) can of coconut milk

rice or flatbreads, to serve

Toss the chicken and 1 teaspoon each of the curry powder and paprika (reserving the rest for the sauce) in a bowl until well coated. If you want to have a more flavourful dish, heat a large, non-stick, heavy-based frying pan over a high heat and add the oil. Add the chicken in an even layer, trying not to overlap the meat, and cook until the chicken has gained some lovely colour on the outside, but not fully cooked (see p12). If you want to skip the frying, you can! Leave the chicken in the spices in the fridge until needed.

Top and tail the onion, removing the dry outer skin. Using a box grater, coarsely grate the onion. Flip the box grater around, then peel and finely grate the garlic. Add the butter to the slow cooker pot and turn on to HIGH. Once the butter has melted, add the onion and garlic and cook for 10 minutes before adding the remaining curry powder and smoked paprika and cooking for 20 minutes with the lid on.

Meanwhile, mix the peanut butter, soy sauce, and stock cube in a medium bowl. Slowly pour in the coconut milk and whisk to create a smooth sauce. Once the onion and spices have been cooking for 30 minutes, add the sauce and the chicken, ensuring you add any resting juices, if using the pan-fried meat. Cook for 3 hours on HIGH or 6 hours on LOW until the sauce has thickened slightly and is smelling aromatic.

This dish pairs really well with rice or flatbreads to soak up the delicious curry sauce.

♡ **Love your leftovers**

Any leftovers will keep well for 2–3 days in the fridge, or freeze for up to 3 months. Defrost and reheat in a saucepan over a medium heat until bubbling and piping hot throughout, adding a touch more water if needed.

Fakeaway

Beef korma	107
Chinese-style spare ribs	108
Sweet and sour pork	111
Lamb curry	112
Garlic teriyaki chicken noodles	114
Chinese-style mushroom curry	117
Chinese-style broccoli beef	118
Easy chicken and mushroom shawarma	121

Using your slow cooker is a brilliant way to make delicious meals that taste just like restaurant takeaways, but are healthier and cheaper, too. Just throw all the ingredients into your slow cooker pot in the morning and then by dinner you'll have a tasty meal for minimal effort. Why not try Chinese-style spare ribs for an easy Friday night fakeaway?

Meat swaps
This korma can also be made with diced chicken thighs or breast, diced lamb shoulder, or diced root veg like butternut squash. Use the same quantities; however, if you're using veg there is no need to brown it in the pan beforehand.

Beef korma

My version of this classic has extra veg grated in the sauce. The little ones won't know it's there, but it adds a yummy flavour and an extra bit of nutrition. What I love about a korma is that it involves ground nuts, which are packed full of healthy fats and vitamins.

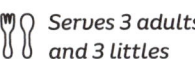 **Serves 3 adults and 3 littles**

 Prep 10 mins, Cook 3-6 hours

Ingredients

1 tbsp sunflower oil

600–800g (1lb 5oz–1lb 12oz) diced stewing beef* (see note)

1 low-salt chicken or vegetable stock cube*

1 large onion

2 courgettes (zucchini)

150ml (⅔ cup) plain yogurt or double (heavy) cream*

60g (⅔ cup) ground almonds

2 garlic cloves, crushed

2 tsp ginger purée

2 tbsp tomato purée (paste)

2 tsp mild curry powder

2 tsp garam masala (a mild blend)

1 tsp ground turmeric

1 tsp ground cumin

1 tsp sugar (optional)

freshly ground black pepper

coriander (cilantro), to serve (optional)

Set a large frying pan over a high heat and add the sunflower oil. Fill your kettle and put it on to boil. Add the meat to the hot pan and cook for 2–3 minutes, tossing once or twice, until browned (see p12). If your frying pan is small, do this in 2 batches.

Meanwhile, crumble the stock cube into a jug. Pour over 250ml (generous 1 cup) of boiling water from the kettle, stir to dissolve, and set aside.

Grate the onion and courgettes on a box grater, or use a food processor to pulse until finely chopped. Add these to the slow cooker along with any juices, the yogurt or cream, and ground almonds.

Tip the browned meat into the slow cooker pot, then place the pan with the meat juices over the heat. Add the garlic and the ginger and tomato purées and cook for 30–60 seconds. Add the curry powder, garam masala, turmeric, cumin, and some black pepper. Stir and cook for a further 30 seconds.

Pour in the stock and deglaze the frying pan by using a wooden spoon to scrape up any lumps stuck to the bottom. Pour the liquid from the pan into the slow cooker, add the sugar, if using, then give it all a good stir. Pop the lid on the slow cooker and cook on LOW for 6 hours or HIGH for 3–4 hours.

Once the meat is tender, give the korma a stir – if it looks slightly separated, don't worry, it just needs stirring together. Serve with rice or flatbreads and fresh coriander, if you like. Plus a little seasoning for the adult portions.

 Love your leftovers

Leftovers will keep for up to 3 days in the fridge, or freeze for up to 2 months. Reheat in the microwave on HIGH from chilled or in a saucepan until piping hot. Or blast in the microwave from frozen for 3–4 minutes until fully defrosted and piping hot throughout.

Chinese-style spare ribs

Super soft pork ribs coated in a sticky sauce delicately flavoured with Chinese spices; for such minimal effort, you'll be surprised at how delicious these are! As the meat is incredibly soft, they are perfect for serving to little taste testers.

 Serves 2 adults and 3 littles

 Prep 30 minutes, Cook 4–7 hours

Ingredients

150ml (⅔ cup) low-sugar and low-salt ketchup

1 tsp Chinese five-spice powder

1 tbsp soft brown sugar (optional)

1 x 90g (3¼oz) pouch of apple purée

4 garlic cloves, minced

1 tsp ground ginger

1 tbsp cornflour (cornstarch)

2 tbsp sesame seeds

1 low-salt chicken stock cube*

1kg (2lb 4oz) pork spare ribs, cut between each bone

freshly ground black pepper

Add the ketchup, five-spice powder, sugar, if using, apple purée, garlic, ginger, cornflour, sesame seeds, and a little black pepper to the slow cooker pot. Crumble in the stock cube and mix really well.

Add the ribs, stirring again to coat the meat well in the sauce. Arrange the ribs so they sit in an even layer in the sauce, which will help them to cook evenly. Pop the lid on and cook on HIGH for 4 hours or LOW for 6–7 hours.

Once done, they are ready and delicious to eat straight away. However, to take the ribs to the next level, I urge you to take one more step. Preheat your oven to 200°C fan (220°C/425°F/Gas 7) and line a very large baking tray with non-stick foil.

Using tongs, or 2 forks, carefully transfer the ribs to the baking tray, spacing them out. Be careful at this stage as the meat is really tender and falls apart easily.

Use a rubber spatula to give the remaining sauce in your slow cooker a really good stir, then spoon a generous amount onto each rib, coating the top side completely.

Place the tray in the preheated oven and bake for 15–20 minutes until the edges have charred slightly and the heat has caramelized the sugars in the sauce, bringing out the flavour. Serve the ribs with oven chips and a side salad for the ultimate home takeaway!

For little ones under 2, let the ribs cool slightly, then pull the meat away from the bone. Ensure you have removed any cartilage – a slight squeeze with your fingers on any meat serving to baby will determine if there are any lumps inside.

 Love your leftovers

The ribs will keep in the fridge for 2 days, or freeze for 3 months. Defrost, then reheat in the oven for 10–15 minutes until piping hot throughout.

Meat swaps
If you want an alternative to pork, you can swap it for diced chicken thighs or stewing steak (beef). Root veggies like butternut squash also work; however, don't use maple syrup if you choose this option as they are already sweet. The veggies won't need to be seared in the pan first.

Sweet and sour pork

Make your own fakeaway at home with this popular, gloriously flavoursome Chinese dish. Many traditional recipes use a lot of added sugar to achieve that sweet element, but this version uses pineapple juice for a healthier option, making it suitable for all ages.

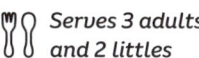

Serves 3 adults and 2 littles

Prep 10 minutes, Cook 3-6 hours

Ingredients

1 tbsp garlic-infused oil

approx. 700g (1lb 9oz) diced pork shoulder*

2 tbsp cornflour (cornstarch)

For the sauce

1 red pepper, deseeded and roughly chopped

1 yellow pepper, deseeded and roughly chopped

1 onion, cut into quarters

2 garlic cloves, crushed

3 tbsp low-sugar and low-salt tomato ketchup

3 tbsp apple cider vinegar

1 x 435g (15oz) can of pineapple chunks in juice

2 tbsp low-salt soy sauce*

1 tbsp maple syrup (optional)

1½ tbsp cornflour

Set a large, non-stick frying pan over a high heat on the hob. Add the garlic oil and let it heat up until very hot.

Coat the diced pork in the 2 tablespoons cornflour (in the open packet the meat came in) to save washing up.

Add the pork to the hot frying pan and spread the chunks into an even single layer – you may need to do this in 2 batches to avoid overcrowding the pan, which will make the pork stew rather than fry. Cook for 3 minutes without touching the pan to get some nice colour on the outside of the pork, then toss and cook for a further 1–2 minutes until browned all over (see p12).

Meanwhile, make the sauce. Add the chopped peppers and onion to the slow cooker pot, followed by 200ml (scant 1 cup) of cold water, the crushed garlic cloves, tomato ketchup, apple cider vinegar, the can of pineapple chunks along with the juice, soy sauce, and maple syrup, if using.

In a separate small bowl or mug, mix the remaining cornflour with a small splash of cold tap water to form a thin paste, then pour this into the slow cooker too.

Add the browned meat to the slow cooker. Stir very well before popping the lid on and cooking for 3 hours on HIGH or 4–6 hours on LOW.

Serve over rice or noodles.

Lamb curry

This rich curry is one to look forward to all day while it cooks away in your kitchen. Perfect with flatbreads for dipping into the creamy sauce.

 Serves 2 adults and 2 littles

 Prep 15 minutes, Cook 6 hours

Ingredients

600g (1lb 5oz) lamb shoulder

1 tbsp sunflower oil

2 large garlic cloves

a thumb-sized piece of fresh ginger

1 medium onion

1 tsp ground turmeric

2 tsp mild garam masala

1 tbsp smoked paprika

1 x 400g (14oz) can of finely chopped tomatoes or passata (strained tomatoes)

150g (⅔ cup) Greek yogurt*

1 low-salt chicken stock cube*

3 tbsp very thick cream*

Cut the meat into bite-sized chunks and trim off most of the fat – if there is a little left, that is totally fine.

Add the oil to a large non-stick frying pan and fry the lamb in batches until charred on the edges. If you cook it all together, then it will stew and you won't get the browned edges that give your curry extra flavour (see p12). Transfer each batch of meat to the slow cooker pot as you go, and repeat until it's all done.

While the meat fries, prep the aromatics. Peel the garlic and ginger, then finely grate to a purée. Coarsely grate the onion.

Once all the meat has been transferred to the slow cooker, add the grated onion to the frying pan to soak up the last of the lamb juices in the base of the pan. Fry for 2–3 minutes to soften the onion, adding a tiny splash of water if the pan feels too dry and the onion is catching. Add the garlic and ginger purée, along with the spices and cook for 1–2 minutes, adding a touch more water if needed. It's important not to burn the spices, but toasting them here will release their flavours and give your curry a stronger flavour.

Add the tomatoes and yogurt to the onion paste and stir it all together, then pour it into the slow cooker pot, using a spatula to ensure you transfer every last bit of the sauce. Crumble in the stock cube, stir, and pop the lid on. Cook for around 6 hours on LOW.

Forty minutes before the end of the cooking time, add the thick cream; this softens the flavour and gives the curry a lovely rich texture.

Serve the curry with rice, naan breads, and veg. For little ones, serve large pieces of meat as finger food, or mash it into the sauce.

 Love your leftovers

The curry will keep for 3 days in the fridge, or freeze for 2 months. Reheat in a saucepan until piping hot and bubbling.

Tip
Swap the lamb for chicken or root veg, like butternut squash, for an alternative flavour. These will take less cooking, so reduce the time by 2 hours, or cook until tender.

Garlic teriyaki chicken noodles

Based on a traditional teriyaki sauce, this recipe calls for much less salty soy sauce and sugar, making it perfect for all the family, but trust me, you'll love this one just as much as your local takeaway. I love to cook this for my Nina, who isn't a fan of mushrooms, as they kind of melt into the sauce and aren't as noticeable in the finished dish.

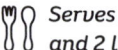 **Serves 2 adults and 2 littles**

 Prep 10 minutes, Cook 3 hours

Ingredients

1 low-salt chicken stock cube*

150g (5½oz) button or chestnut mushrooms

350g (12oz) boneless, skinless chicken thighs

3 tbsp very low-salt soy sauce*

1 tbsp sesame oil

1 tbsp honey or sugar (optional)

3 large garlic cloves

50g (3½ tbsp) cornflour (cornstarch), plus extra 1 tbsp for a thicker sauce

200g (7oz) egg noodles*

freshly ground black pepper

Boil the kettle and crumble the stock cube into the slow cooker pot. Measure out 300ml (1¼ cups) of boiling water and add to the pot, stirring to help the stock cube dissolve.

Use a box grater to grate the mushrooms or chop finely using a knife. Add to the slow cooker too, along with the chicken, soy sauce, sesame oil, a grinding of pepper, and the honey if using.

On the fine side of the box grater, finely grate the garlic, you should be left with a generous tablespoon of garlic. Add this to the slow cooker.

Add the cornflour to a bowl, then add 50ml (scant ¼ cup) of cold water, stir to make a smooth paste, and pour into the pot. Stir well and ensure the chicken is lying flat and submerged in the liquid. Pop the lid on and cook for 3 hours on HIGH.

Once done, take the lid off and give it all a good stir to break up the chicken a little. The sauce should be dark and thickened and the meat falling apart easily.

If you would prefer a thicker sauce, mix the extra 1 tablespoon of cornflour with a splash of water and stir into the sauce. Put the lid on and cook on HIGH until your noodles are ready. But do note that when you add the noodles it will feel like a thicker sauce.

Cook the noodles according to the packet instructions, then drain very well to avoid thinning down the sauce too much. Add to the chicken, stir well using tongs, and serve. Delicious with a scattering of sesame seeds and veggies on the side. Adults you can add some chilli sauce and more soy sauce, if you wish.

 Love your leftovers

Leftovers will keep in the fridge for 4 days. I like to pop these in the air fryer for 5 minutes to reheat. They will also freeze well for 2 months. Cook in the oven from frozen for 8–10 minutes until piping hot.

Chinese-style mushroom curry

Mushrooms are slow-cooked until silky soft in this mild Chinese-style curry sauce, making for a simple yet delicious meal. Feel free to replace the chestnut mushrooms with 6 diced chicken thighs or a cubed butternut squash for a little more variety.

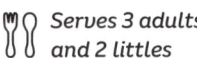

Serves 3 adults and 2 littles

Prep 8 minutes, Cook 2-4 hours

Ingredients

250g (9oz) button mushrooms

1 brown onion

2 heaped tbsp cornflour (cornstarch)

2 large garlic cloves, minced or crushed

1½ tsp ground turmeric

1 low-salt chicken or vegetable stock cube*, crumbled

2 tsp mild curry powder

2 tbsp low-salt soy sauce*

2 large handfuls of frozen peas

500g (1lb 2oz) chestnut mushrooms (or extra button mushrooms)

1 x 400g (14oz) can of coconut milk

a little freshly ground black pepper

Grate the button mushrooms and the onion on a box grater, or pulse them in a food processor until finely chopped.

Add the onion and mushroom pulp and any escaping juices to the slow cooker pot. Add the cornflour, garlic, turmeric, crumbled stock cube, curry powder, soy sauce, frozen peas, and a little black pepper.

Either quarter the chestnut mushrooms or cut them into chunky strips (which may be easier for little ones under 2 to hold and eat), then add these to the slow cooker too. Give everything a good stir to dissolve the cornflour. Stir in the coconut milk, then quarter-fill the empty can with cold tap water to swill out any remaining coconut milk and add this to the pot.

Pop the lid on and cook for 2 hours on HIGH or for 3–4 hours on LOW. Serve with naan bread or over rice to soak up all the delicious sauce. Adults may want an extra dash of soy sauce or a sprinkling of salt.

Note If you're serving to under 1s, they may struggle with the chunks of mushroom, so grate a higher proportion of your mushrooms, or alternatively, blend up their sauce a little.

♡ Love your leftovers

Leftovers will keep in the fridge for up to 3 days. Reheat in a saucepan until piping hot and bubbling. This dish will also freeze for up to 3 months. Defrost at room temperature and reheat as above, or defrost and reheat in the microwave for 3–4 minutes until piping hot throughout.

Chinese-style broccoli beef

Succulent beef and nutritious broccoli in a flavourful Chinese-style sauce. This is so quick to whip up at lunchtime, you'll feel smug all afternoon knowing dinner will be a doddle!

 Serves 2 adults and 2 littles

 Prep 7 minutes, Cook 2-4 hours

Ingredients

2 low-salt beef or vegetable stock cubes*

600g (1lb 5oz) stewing steak (beef)

1½ tsp sesame oil

3 tbsp low-salt soy sauce*

4 garlic cloves, minced

2 tbsp sesame seeds, plus 1 tbsp extra to serve

2 tsp sugar (optional)

2 heaped tbsp cornflour (cornstarch)

1 large head of broccoli, cut into large florets

thinly sliced spring onion (scallion), to garnish (optional)

Boil the kettle, then add 700ml (scant 3 cups) of boiling water to a measuring jug. Crumble in the stock cubes and stir to dissolve them.

Cut the steak into 1.5cm (⅝in) wide strips. Add the meat to the slow cooker pot along with the hot beef stock, sesame oil, soy sauce, garlic, sesame seeds, and sugar, if using. Stir the ingredients together well and pop the lid on. Cook for 4 hours on LOW or for 2–3 hours on HIGH.

Once the beef is tender, add the cornflour to a small mug, then add around 3–4 tablespoons of cold tap water and stir to make a runny paste. Add this to the slow cooker and stir well. Add the broccoli and stir once more before putting the lid back on and cooking for another 30–35 minutes on HIGH until the sauce has thickened and the broccoli has cooked.

Serve over noodles or rice with the extra 1 tablespoon of sesame seeds scattered over. Garnish with sliced spring onion, if you like.

 Love your leftovers

Leftovers (without rice or noodles) will keep for up to 2 days in the fridge. Reheat in the microwave for 2–3 minutes on HIGH or in a saucepan until piping hot throughout. Once cooled completely, you can also freeze the broccoli beef for up to 2 months. Defrost thoroughly and reheat as above.

Tip
Shred the chicken with a fork if you want the pieces to be smaller for little ones.

Easy chicken and mushroom shawarma

A real family sharing meal, perfect to let the kids help themselves and decide how they want to construct their plate. Leave out the mushrooms if they don't float your boat.

 Serves 2 adults and 2 littles

 Prep 20 minutes, Cook 3-4 hours

Ingredients

4 large flat mushrooms

6 skinless, boneless chicken thighs

1 tbsp smoked paprika

1 heaped tsp ground cumin

½ tsp ground cinnamon

1 tsp ground turmeric

1 heaped tbsp cornflour (cornstarch)

3 fat garlic cloves, finely grated

finely grated zest and juice of 1 unwaxed lemon

3 tbsp garlic-infused olive oil or regular olive oil

freshly ground black pepper

For the garlic dip

4 heaped tbsp plain Greek yogurt*

1 small garlic clove, finely minced

juice of 1 lemon

To serve

favourite chopped salad bits, such as cucumber, peppers, shredded lettuce, tomatoes, onions, pickled cabbage, pickled gherkins; pitta breads or tortilla wraps*, warmed in the oven, if wished; hot sauce

Chop the large flat mushrooms into thick strips and the chicken thighs in half. Put the chicken and mushrooms in a large sealable food bag along with the spices, cornflour, garlic, lemon zest and juice, 2 tablespoons of the garlic oil and a little pepper. Seal the bag and give it a good mix – it may help to release some of the air from inside the bag. Squeeze the chicken around the bag with your hands – this not only helps to coat the chicken in all the spices, but also helps tenderize the meat a little. You can now bake this straightaway, or marinate in the fridge for up to 24 hours.

When you are ready to cook, add the remaining tablespoon of oil to the slow cooker and heat the oil for 5 minutes on HIGH. Lay the chicken flat in one even layer. If you like, you can quickly sear the chicken in a frying pan over a medium-high heat until slightly charred (see p.12), then add it to your slow cooker. This is an extra step, but will add more flavour to the dish!

Once the chicken is in the slow cooker, cook on HIGH for 1 hour with the lid off. After 1 hour, use tongs to turn the chicken and nestle the mushrooms around the meat. Pour in any spiced marinade from the mushroom bag along with 2–3 tablespoons of boiling water. Pop the lid on and cook for 2 hours on HIGH. If it is looking very dry, add a teaspoon of water. After this time, remove the lid and cook for 30 minutes with the lid off.

Mix all the dip ingredients together in a small bowl and season with a little black pepper. Prepare the salad and arrange, with the pickles, on a platter or in bowls. Once the chicken is cooked, remove from the slow cooker and allow to rest for 5 minutes before slicing into 1.5cm (⅝in) wide strips. Place 2 pitta breads at the bottom of a serving bowl and tip the chicken and mushrooms on top, including any juices from the slow cooker. All these yummy juices will soak into the bread – my absolute favourite part! Serve with hot sauce for the adults.

 Love your leftovers

Any leftovers can be kept in the fridge for 2 days and are truly delicious cold in a tortilla wrap – lunchbox goals!

Weekend Favourites

Pulled pork	127
Lamb tagine	128
Pulled chicken tikka	131
Jacket potatoes with cheesy chilli	132
Gammon in a mustard glaze	136
Sunday dinner pork belly	139
Tropical rice pudding	140
Banana peach cake	143
Fruity crumble	144
Winter-spiced poached plums and pears	147
Hot mulled apple juice	148

The weekend is about being with family and spending minimal time in the kitchen, so why not make use of your slow cooker? All the recipes in this chapter are easy to put together and will be real winners with all your family. I've even included some desserts, such as a delicious Fruity crumble when you fancy something sweet and a Hot mulled apple juice for a warming winter treat.

Pulled pork

GF* EF DF*

Don't be alarmed by this list of ingredients; use what you already have in your spice rack – it's going to be delicious, trust me! This is great served in a burger bun, or in a toasted sandwich or wrap. Serve alongside a small bowl of the meat juices to dip your sarnie into. You can also use the meat to make lasagne or bulk out pasta dishes. But my favourite way is to get messy and make pulled pork tacos, served with a slaw.

  Serves 6

 Prep 10 minutes, Cook 4–8 hours

Ingredients

1 tbsp smoked paprika

2 tsp garlic granules

1 tsp ground cumin

2 tsp dried mixed herbs

2 heaped tsp plain (all-purpose) flour*

1.5–2kg (3lb 5oz–4lb 8oz) pork shoulder, string removed

1 tbsp sunflower oil

1 low-salt chicken stock cube*

2 tsp mustard (optional)

2 tbsp Worcestershire sauce (optional)

2 tbsp apple cider vinegar

1 heaped tbsp soft brown sugar (optional)

4 tbsp low-sugar and low-salt ketchup

1 tbsp low-salt soy sauce*

1 large onion, halved

1 small garlic bulb, halved crossways

Put the smoked paprika, garlic granules, ground cumin, and dried herbs in a small bowl. Stir well, then spoon half of this spice mix onto a plate along with the flour and mix the spices into the flour. Roll the pork in the spiced flour so that it is coated on all sides.

Set a large frying pan over a high heat and add the oil. Lay the pork in the centre and cook hard and fast on all sides to generate some dark colour and crispiness on the outside of the pork. This will add flavour and help the pork to stay super juicy (see p12).

Meanwhile, add the remaining spice mix to a large jug with 300ml (1¼ cups) boiling water from the kettle. Crumble the stock cube and add it to the jug along with the mustard, Worcestershire sauce, vinegar, sugar, if using, ketchup, and soy sauce. Give it all a good mix and add it to the slow cooker pot along with the onion, garlic bulb, and pork. Pop the lid on and cook for 4–5 hours on HIGH or for 8 hours on LOW.

Once the meat is really tender and breaks away easily, it is done. Transfer the meat to a large bowl and use 2 forks to shred it up. Take the onion out of the sauce and discard. Squeeze the garlic cloves out, discarding the skin, and mash the soft garlic into the sauce. Then add the shredded meat back to the cooking juices and give it a good mix.

You're now ready to enjoy this meat however you like; I love it in tacos. For this, toast a couple of mini wraps in a frying pan or over an open flame on a gas burner, then mound up a little pile of the pulled pork and some slaw on the taco, fold over, and enjoy! For little ones, it'll be easier for them to enjoy this meal deconstructed.

 Love your leftovers

Pulled pork leftovers will keep really well for 2–3 days in the fridge, or 3 months in the freezer. When reheating in a saucepan or microwave, ensure it is piping hot throughout before serving.

Lamb tagine

GF* **EF** **DF***

With tender lamb, rich sauce and Moroccan flavours of cumin, cinnamon, and chickpeas, this throw-it-all-in recipe is the perfect comfort food on a cold, wintery day.

 Serves 2 adults and 3 littles

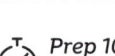 **Prep 10 minutes, Cook 4-7 hours**

Ingredients

2 tbsp sunflower oil

750g (1lb 10oz) lamb shoulder, diced and most of the excess fat removed

1 large brown onion

3 large carrots

2 tsp ground cumin

2 tsp sweet paprika

1 x 400g (14oz) can of chickpeas in water, drained

1 x 400g (14oz) can of chopped tomatoes

2 low-salt chicken or beef stock cubes*, crumbled

2 large garlic cloves, crushed

½ tsp ground cinnamon

a handful of seedless raisins (optional)

fresh herbs, to garnish (optional)

Set a large frying pan over a high heat and add 1 tablespoon of the sunflower oil. Fill the kettle and put it on to boil.

Once the oil is hot, add half of the lamb to the pan, spread it out in an even layer, and leave to fry for 2 minutes until the outside of the meat is nicely browned. Use a spatula to turn the meat over and leave to fry for a further 1–2 minutes (see p12). Transfer the browned meat to the slow cooker pot and repeat the browning process with the remaining lamb.

Meanwhile, grate or finely dice the onion, peel the carrots and cut them into chunks. Add these to the slow cooker, along with the rest of the ingredients.

When all the meat is browned and in the slow cooker, add 400ml (1⅔ cups) of boiling water from the kettle to the empty hot frying pan. Stir with a wooden spoon for 30 seconds to let the water soak up any caramelized bits of meat from the base of the pan, as this is where the flavour is. Pour this flavoured water into the slow cooker.

Give it all a really good stir and pop the lid on. Cook for 4 hours on HIGH or for 6–7 hours on LOW until the meat is super tender.

Serve in big bowls with boiled potatoes to soak up all the juices and fresh herbs to garnish, if you like. Chickpeas are usually too small to be a hazard for little taste testers; however, feel free to mash them with a fork before serving, if you prefer.

 Love your leftovers

Leftovers will keep for up to 2 days in the fridge. Reheat in a saucepan until bubbling and piping hot throughout. Or, you can freeze the tagine for up to 2 months and defrost thoroughly before reheating as above.

Veggie swaps
Swap the chicken for butternut squash or aubergine (eggplant) cubes for a veg-filled curry instead. For extra protein, try adding some cooked canned lentils too.

Pulled chicken tikka

The throw it-all-in kinda dish that we crave on busy days! Serve over rice or with potatoes, or how about even using the pulled chicken as a filling for a different take on lasagne? Any leftovers are also delicious in a warmed wrap or toasted panini.

 Serves 2 adults and 2 littles

 Prep 5 minutes, Cook 4 hours

Ingredients

1 onion

1 tsp very mild chilli powder (or as hot as your family like it)

1 tsp ground turmeric

1 tsp ground coriander

1 tsp ground cumin

2 tbsp smoked paprika

2 tbsp sweet paprika

2 tsp mild garam masala

3 garlic cloves, crushed

2 tbsp garlic-infused oil

2 tbsp tomato purée (paste)

6 skinless, boneless chicken thighs or 4 chicken breasts*

2–3 heaped tbsp thick Greek yogurt or double (heavy) cream* (optional)

freshly ground black pepper

Chop the top off the onion, but leave the root attached. Peel off the skin and pull it over the root where it is still connected. Use the attached onion skin as your handle to hold the onion while you grate the flesh using the coarse side of a box grater.

Add the grated onion pulp and any juice to the slow cooker pot, along with all the spices, the garlic, garlic oil, tomato purée, and a generous grinding of black pepper. Mix well, then add the chicken before mixing again.

Put the lid on and cook for 3–4 hours on LOW, or until the chicken is very tender and shreds easily. Using a wooden spoon, mix the chicken firmly into the sauce to shred it up – it should be so soft that it easily falls apart.

This is delicious to eat as it is now, but you can also add some Greek yogurt or a splash of double cream to turn this into a creamy curry.

 Love your leftovers

Leftovers will keep for up to 3 days in the fridge. To reheat, pop in the microwave for 2–3 minutes on HIGH, or heat in a lidded saucepan for 5–10 minutes until piping hot throughout. You can also freeze this for up to 2 months. Defrost and reheat in the microwave for 3–4 minutes on HIGH, or defrost in the fridge, then reheat as above.

Jacket potatoes with cheesy chilli

 Fills 4 large jacket potatoes

 Prep 20 minutes, Cook 4-8 hours

GF
EF
DF

A family staple in my house all year round. Baked potatoes are such a comforting meal – perfect to have on in the background while you can take the time to make a cheesy chilli that the kids will love.

Firstly, choose nice large baking potatoes. Wash them well and if they are particularly dirty, give them a little scrub with a potato brush. Pat dry with kitchen paper, prick 5 or 6 times all over each potato to allow the steam to escape and avoid exploding, then rub them with a touch of oil. Wrap each pricked and oiled potato in a square of foil and place them in the slow cooker pot in a single layer. Pop the lid on and cook on HIGH for 4 hours or LOW for 7–8 hours.

Meanwhile, for the chilli, put the mince and oil into a large saucepan over a medium–high heat. Dice the onion quickly and add that to the pan too, then, using a wooden spoon, break up the mince into small pieces. Cook for 5 minutes, or until the onions are soft and the mince has turned brown (see p12).

Ingredients

4 large baking potatoes

regular olive or garlic-infused olive oil

For the cheesy chilli

500g (1lb 2oz) lean minced (ground) beef

1 tsp sunflower or garlic-infused oil

1 small onion

2 large garlic cloves

2 tbsp tomato purée (paste)

1 x 400g (14oz) can of haricot or kidney beans in water, drained and roughly mashed

1 small can of sweetcorn in water

1 low-salt beef stock cube*

500g (1lb 2oz) tomato passata (strained tomatoes)

2 tbsp smoked paprika

1 tsp dried mixed herbs

½ tsp ground cumin

80g (2¾oz) smoked Cheddar cheese*, finely grated, plus extra to serve

To serve

butter or dairy-free spread

sour cream

avocado

Serving to little ones
You can either cut the potato into finger strips, or mash the potato with the back of a fork, then spoon some chilli over the top and add a little sour cream and avocado.

Meanwhile, mince the garlic, then add to the pan, along with the tomato purée. Cook for a further 2 minutes before draining the beans and sweetcorn and adding those to the pan too. Crumble in the stock cube, then add the passata, smoked paprika, dried herbs, and cumin. Quarter fill the passata carton with water, swill around to catch all the remaining tomato juice, and add to the pan. Stir everything together well, then put the lid on and cook for at least 20 minutes, but even up to an hour over a low heat is perfect.

Before serving the chilli, take it off the heat and stir in the cheese, allowing it to melt into the sauce. To serve, cut the potatoes into quarters, keeping the base still attached, and add a dollop of butter or dairy-free spread and the chilli to the centre with a little sour cream, avocado, and extra cheese on top.

 Love your leftovers

The chilli will keep in the fridge for 3 days, or freeze for 3 months. Once defrosted, reheat in a saucepan until piping hot.

Gammon in a mustard glaze

GF* EF DF*

Soft and tender meat that just falls apart with a fork, coated in a delicious mustard glaze, and crisped up in the oven for maximum flavour, this is a real showstopper for your Sunday family roast and is my Christmas Eve tradition! This recipe has a few different spices that help give the gammon its flavour, but will still be amazing without, so if you would like to leave them out, don't let it stop you from making this one.

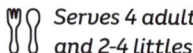 **Serves 4 adults and 2-4 littles**

 Prep 40 minutes, Cook 3-6 hours

Ingredients

2kg (4lb 8oz) joint of smoked gammon (with a layer of fat on the outside)

1 brown onion

1 garlic bulb

½ tsp coriander seeds (optional)

2–3 allspice berries (optional)

2 juniper berries (optional)

4 cloves (optional)

1 tsp black peppercorns

For the glaze

2 tbsp wholegrain mustard (optional)

1 tbsp Dijon mustard (optional)

2 tbsp honey (if planning on serving to under 1s, use maple syrup instead)

freshly ground black pepper

Put the gammon joint into your slow cooker pot with the strings or casing (not the plastic packaging) still attached as this will hold it together as it cooks. Cut the onion in half and top and tail the garlic bulb to expose the ends of the cloves and add these too. Add all of the spices and pour in enough water to come a quarter of the way up the side of the joint. Put the lid on and cook for 6 hours on LOW or for 3–4 hours on HIGH.

Once the gammon is almost cooked, line a baking tray with non-stick foil and preheat the oven to 220°C fan (240°C/475°F/Gas 8) – the hotter the better as you want to really caramelize the crust. Carefully lift the joint out of the slow cooker using 2 large forks and place on the prepared baking tray. Allow to cool a little while you prepare the glaze.

Mix all the glaze ingredients together in a bowl and season with a good grind of black pepper. Remove any strings or outer casing from the meat and gently rotate the joint so that the fatty section is facing up. If your joint has the skin on it too, carefully remove this, leaving a layer of fat still attached to the joint. Using a knife, score a criss-cross pattern into the fat, ensuring not to cut through into the meat. Pour the glaze over the joint, using the back of a spoon to spread it evenly across the entire top side of the joint. Quickly put the gammon in the oven before all of the glaze drips down the sides. Bake for 15–25 minutes or until the top has turned deliciously dark and crispy, using a spoon once or twice during cooking to baste the joint with the glaze at the bottom of the pan. Remove from the oven and allow to rest for at least 15 minutes before serving.

♡ Love your leftovers

Gammon is one of my favourite things to have in the fridge: use in sandwiches; dice and toss through pasta; use it to top pizza; or cook into an omelette – the possibilities are endless. It will keep for 5–7 days in the fridge, or freeze for 1–2 months. Defrost fully before reheating until piping hot in the oven or a frying pan.

Tip
Gammon is a salty piece of meat, therefore it is advised to only offer a very small amount to taste for little ones under 1 – exposure and variety is a great thing.

Sunday dinner pork belly

Pork is one of the cheaper meat options for a Sunday roast, and great for serving a large crowd. Super soft juicy tender meat with gorgeous pork crackling, serve with gravy, steamed broccoli, and roast carrots and potatoes.

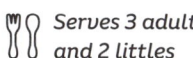

Serves 3 adults and 2 littles

Prep 10 minutes, Cook 2-3 hours

Ingredients

800g (1lb 12oz) slab of pork belly with the rind still attached

1 tsp peppercorns from the grinder

6 garlic cloves

1 tsp oil

1 tsp dried mixed herbs

salt

Bring the meat up to room temperature while you pat the skin dry with some kitchen paper. Add the pork, flat and unravelled, to a slow cooker pot, with the fatty skin-side facing up. Then add the peppercorns and garlic, no need to peel the cloves. Ensure that you place them down the sides of the pork and not on the skin.

Add enough cold water to just cover the meat, but not the fatty line under the skin. It's important that you don't splash the water onto the skin, so gently pour it into the slow cooker down the sides to keep the skin as dry as possible for a crispier finish later.

Place the lid on and cook for 1 hour 40 minutes–2 hours on HIGH until the meat is tender. You can also cook for 4 hours on LOW if you'd prefer.

Take a large piece of foil and lay it over a baking sheet. In the centre, add the oil and a sprinkling of herbs, roughly the same size as the meat. Carefully remove the meat from the slow cooker using a fish slice. Let any juice drop into the slow cooker for a second before transferring the pork over and placing on the herby oil. Fold and roll the excess foil in 4cm (1½in) sections towards the meat, then scrunch or fold the ends together to form a little open-topped box for the pork to sit in, with the fatty skin on top completely exposed. Use kitchen paper to pat the skin dry again; it'll feel sticky to touch, which is what you want. Add a liberal coating of salt to just the skin, which will help it crisp up. If you're serving to little ones, don't worry – it will just be the crackling for adults that is salty, the soft meat underneath will be untouched.

Allow it to sit to one side for 15 minutes so the skin can dry out further, and preheat the grill to 180°C (350°F).

Once hot, grill the meat directly under the heat for 20 minutes until the crackling has turned crispy and bubbled up. Keep an eye on it, and rotate the meat if necessary for an even grilling. Serve in slices, with the fatty line removed for little ones.

Tropical rice pudding

This comforting dessert brings a little sunshine to your day with flavours of coconut, pineapple, and peach. Whack it all in the slow cooker in the afternoon and enjoy a delicious no-added-sugar treat after dinner.

Makes 6 small portions

Prep 5 minutes, Cook 2½–6 hours

Ingredients

30g (1oz) unsalted soft butter*, for greasing

160g (¾ cup) pudding rice

1 x 400g (14oz) can of coconut milk

550ml (scant 2½ cups) milk*

2 tsp vanilla extract

1 x 425g (15oz) can of pineapple chunks in juice

1 x 415g (14¾oz) can of peach slices in juice

fresh fruit, to serve (optional)

demerara sugar, to serve (optional)

Generously grease the bottom and sides of your slow cooker pot with butter to avoid the rice pudding sticking.

Put all of the ingredients, including the juice from the cans of fruit, into the slow cooker and give it a little stir to combine. Put the lid on and cook for 2½–3½ hours on HIGH or 4–6 hours on LOW. It will be ready when the rice feels soft.

When you initially take the lid off, it may seem like the rice pudding has split, but don't worry – use a rubber spatula to give it a really good mix and it will all come together.

Serve in bowls as is, or with a little extra fruit on top or a sprinkling of demerara sugar.

For babies under 12 months, mash the pineapple in their portion gently with a fork to break it up.

 Love your leftovers

The rice pudding will keep for 2 days in the fridge, or freeze for 3 months. Defrost and reheat with an extra splash of milk, as it will really thicken as it cools.

Banana peach cake

 GF*
 DF*
 V

This cake is giving serious comforting vibes. Moist, sweet, and really easy to put together – a great one to get baking before you head out for a walk and return to the best afternoon treat.

Serves 8-10

Prep 10 minutes, Cook 2-2½ hours

Ingredients

1 x 415g (14¾oz) can of peach slices in juice

3 medium ripe bananas

100g (scant ½ cup) unsalted butter*, melted, plus extra (optional) for greasing

2 eggs

1 x 410g (14½oz) can of unsweetened evaporated milk*

2 tsp vanilla extract

70g (⅓ cup) light soft brown or caster sugar (optional)

450g (3⅓ cups) self-raising flour*

1 heaped tsp baking powder*

2 tsp ground cinnamon

Cut a piece of non-stick baking paper to fit neatly in the base of your slow cooker pot. A large slow cooker works best for this recipe, roughly 6.5 litres (27⅓ cups), but slightly smaller will also work. Grease the sides of the slow cooker pot if it's not non-stick. Add the canned peaches evenly to the slow cooker, reserving the liquid for later.

In a mixing bowl, mash the bananas, then add the butter, eggs, evaporated milk, vanilla extract, and sugar, if using. Whisk very well until fully combined. Add 80ml (⅓ cup) of the reserved peach juices, mix again, then add the remaining dry ingredients.

Stir well to form a smooth batter, but be sure to avoid overworking it. Pour the cake batter into the slow cooker, in a thin, even layer over the top of the fruit, to avoid moving the peaches too much and so they stay evenly distributed at the base of the slow cooker.

Take 4 pieces of kitchen paper, all still attached on one long sheet, then fold over in half so you have 2 layers of 2, and place this over the top of the slow cooker, followed by the lid. Gently pull the sides of the paper to ensure it is not sagging in the middle. Cook for 2–2½ hours on HIGH, depending on the size and shape of your slow cooker.

Check after 2 hours and insert a knife into the centre; if it comes out clean with no raw batter stuck to it, then it should be ready. Turn off the slow cooker and let the cake stand with the lid off for 5 minutes. Run a spatula around the edges of the cake, then place a board or serving plate over the slow cooker and turn it over using oven gloves, as the slow cooker pot will be very hot. Allow the cake to cool until just warm, then serve up in slices and enjoy.

 Love your leftovers

Leftovers will store in an airtight container for 2-3 days, or you can freeze for up to 3 months, defrosting at room temperature.

Fruity crumble

There are lots of reasons why a slow cooker is great, and this comforting fruity crumble has to be one of the most surprising. Soft, melt-in-the-mouth fruit topped with a crumbly, almost crisp in parts, topping. It's absolutely glorious with a dash of custard or cream!

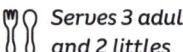

Serves 3 adults and 2 littles

Prep 10 minutes, Cook 3-6 hours

Ingredients

5 red eating apples

6 small ripe plums

2 tsp ground cinnamon

1 tbsp cornflour (cornstarch)

1 x 400g (14oz) can of peach slices in unsweetened juice

150g (scant 1½ cups) rolled porridge oats*

80g (⅔ cup) plain (all-purpose) flour*

1 tsp vanilla extract

90g (generous ⅓ cup) unsalted butter*, melted

40g (scant ¼ cup) light soft brown sugar (optional)

Peel, core, and cut the apples into approx. 2cm (¾in) wide wedges and add these to the slow cooker pot. Halve the plums and remove the stones, then cut them into quarters and add to the apples. Sprinkle the cinnamon and cornflour over the fruit, then stir well to coat the fruit evenly. Pour the entire can of peach slices and their juice over the fruit and stir again.

In a separate bowl, mix together the oats, flour, vanilla extract, melted butter, and brown sugar, if using, until you see no dry oats or flour. Evenly sprinkle the crumble mixture over the fruit, reaching right to the edges of the slow cooker pot.

Take 4 sheets of kitchen paper and place them over the top of the slow cooker pot in a double layer, using more paper if you see any gaps. Place the lid on the slow cooker over the paper. Gently pull the paper so it is fairly taught under the lid and not flopping down into the crumble. The job of this paper is to soak up as much condensation as possible, which should stop the crumble topping from going soggy.

Cook for 3 hours on HIGH or for 5-6 hours on LOW, until the fruit is soft and the crumble topping is crisp. Be careful when you take the lid off as there will be lots of water droplets on it, so quickly move the lid away from the slow cooker to avoid the water dripping back down into the crumble and remove the kitchen paper. If you're at home, you can replace the kitchen paper with fresh sheets halfway through cooking if the pieces of paper sticking out seem saturated. However, don't worry if this isn't convenient, it will be totally fine if you don't replace them.

Serve the warm crumble in bowls with a dash of custard or cream.

Out of kitchen paper?
If you don't have any kitchen paper, you can use a clean, dry tea towel instead. Just ensure you haven't used a strong smelling fabric conditioner, as this will seep into the crumble and give it a funny taste.

Weekend Favourites

Winter-spiced poached plums and pears

A hug in a bowl! The perfect winter pudding, and if you end up with any leftovers, top it on freshly made porridge the next morning... thank me later!

 Serves 2 adults and 2 littles

 Prep 10 minutes, Cook 2 hours

Ingredients

300g (10oz) pears (about 4 pears)

1 cinnamon stick, or 1 heaped tsp ground cinnamon

1 vanilla pod, or 2 tsp pure vanilla extract

40g (3½ tbsp) unrefined sugar, such as maple syrup or golden caster (superfine) sugar (optional)

300g (10oz) plums (about 5–7 plums)

Peel the pears, cut into quarters lengthways, remove the stem, and scoop out the middle core. Add the pears to the slow cooker pot along with the cinnamon, vanilla, maple syrup or sugar, and 200ml (scant 1 cup) cold water. Pop the lid on and cook for 1 hour on LOW.

Meanwhile, quarter (or halve if small) and stone your plums, then add these to the slow cooker pot. Put the lid back on and cook for a further 1 hour. The fruit should be soft while still holding its shape. You may want to cook a little longer, depending on the ripeness of your fruit.

Turn the slow cooker off and serve the fruit with full-fat Greek-style yogurt and lots of the warm juice from the pot. Or, allow to cool and store in the fridge until needed (for up to 3 days).

You can mash for baby or serve as is, as the fruit is really soft.

Transform it!
This is fantastic mashed and served on toast, or double up the quantity and top with a crumble oat topping for a delicious family pudding.

Hot mulled apple juice

The glee in my 4-year-old's face as I handed her a warm cup of this cinnamon-infused, comforting drink. "Oh my goodness Mummy, did you really make this? It's so good!" Well, that's what any parent wants to hear, right?

Makes 6 adult-sized mugs

Prep 10 minutes, Cook 2-3 hours

Ingredients

900ml (3¾ cups) fresh unsweetened apple juice, not from concentrate

1 cinnamon stick

3 red crisp eating apples (optional but adds extra flavour)

1 small orange

GF EF DF V Vg

Add the apple juice, 700ml (scant 3 cups) water, and cinnamon stick to the slow cooker pot. If you are using them, cut the apples into wedges and discard the cores – no need to peel in my opinion. Add these to the slow cooker too.

Use a potato peeler to peel the zest off the orange, taking care to only peel the orange zest and not the white pith attached, as this will make the juice a little bitter. Add the zest to the slow cooker and squeeze the juice of the orange in too, catching any pips in your hands as you do.

Pop the lid on and cook on HIGH for 2–3 hours until hot and smelling delicious. Strain the liquid into mugs to serve. Add a dash of cold water to cool it down for the little ones.

The apples stewed in the juice are delicious served warm over ice cream, or save them for breakfast in the morning to top porridge.

Note The fruit juice in this recipe has been diluted with water; however, I still recommend serving it alongside something to eat so any natural sugars don't sit on the teeth for too long. This rule applies when serving all fruit juices. If you're serving to under 2s, feel free to dilute the juice further with water and serve in moderation.

♡ Love your leftovers

This juice will keep for up to 2–3 days in the fridge. I recommend straining it into a jug to store so that the flavour doesn't become too strong as it sits. You can serve it cold, dilute with a little fizzy water or reheat in the microwave or in a saucepan on the hob. You can also make ice pops out of leftovers and keep them in the freezer for up to 6 months.

Conversions

If required, we recommend you follow the conversions as listed on the individual recipes; however, here is a handy list of standard conversions should you need them for anything else.

VOLUME MEASURES	
75ml	2½fl oz
90ml	3fl oz
100ml	3½fl oz
120ml	4fl oz
150ml	5fl oz
200ml	7fl oz
240ml	8fl oz
250ml	9fl oz
300ml	10fl oz
350ml	12fl oz
400ml	14fl oz
450ml	15fl oz
500ml	16fl oz
600ml	1 pint
750ml	1¼ pints
900ml	1½ pints
1 litre	1¾ pints
1.2 litres	2 pints
1.4 litres	2½ pints
1.5 litres	2¾ pints
1.7 litres	3 pints
2 litres	3½ pints
3 litres	5¼ pints

LENGTH MEASURES	
3mm	⅛in
6mm	¼in
1cm	½in
2cm	¾in
2.5cm	1in
5cm	2in
6cm	2½in
8cm	3in
10cm	4in
13cm	5in
15cm	6in
18cm	7in
20cm	8in
22cm	9in
25cm	10in
28cm	11in
30cm	12in (1ft)

OVEN TEMPERATURES	
130°C	110°C fan/250°F/Gas ½
140°C	120°C fan/275°F/Gas 1
150°C	130°C fan/300°F/Gas 2
160°C	140°C fan/325°F/Gas 3
180°C	160°C fan/350°F/Gas 4
190°C	170°C fan/375°F/Gas 5
200°C	180°C fan/400°F/Gas 6
220°C	200°C fan/425°F/Gas 7
230°C	210°C fan/455°F/Gas 8

AUSTRALIA – UK SPOON MEASURES	
½ tbsp	2 tsp
1 tbsp	1 heaped tbsp
2 tbsp (8 tsp)	2½ tbsp
3 tbsp (12 tsp)	4 tbsp
4 tbsp (16 tsp)	5 tbsp
5 tbsp (20 tsp)	6½ tbsp
6 tbsp (24 tsp)	8 tbsp

DRY MEASURES	
15g	½oz
30g	1oz
60g	2oz
90g	3oz
125g	4oz (¼lb)
155g	5oz
185g	6oz
220g	7oz
250g	8oz (½lb)
280g	9oz
315g	10oz
345g	11oz
375g	12oz (¾lb)
410g	13oz
440g	14oz
470g	15oz
500g	16oz (1lb)
750g	24oz (1½lb)
1kg	32oz (2lb)

Index

Note: page numbers in **bold** refer to illustrations.

A

apple
  fruity crumble 144, **145**
  hot mulled apple juice 148, **149**
  pork and apple orzotto 54, **55**
aubergine
  easy aubergine stew 46, **47**
  Turkish chicken stew **44**, 45

B

bacon, traditional Bolognese **64**, 65
banana 20
  banana peach cake **142**, 143
batch cooking 19
bean(s)
  freezer raid veg stew **40**, 41
  jacket potatoes with cheesy chilli 132–3, **134–5**
  Mexican soup **32**, 33
  smoky pork and bean stew 42, **43**
  Spanish chicken and sweetcorn stew 38, **39**
  turkey chilli **80**, 81
beef
  beef korma **106**, 107
  Chinese-style broccoli beef 118, **119**

hearty goulash soup **28**, 29
hodgepodge shortcut lasagne 68, **69**
jacket potatoes with cheesy chilli 132–3, **134–5**
meatballs in tomato sauce 56–7, **58–9**
Mexican soup **32**, 33
proper beef stew and dumplings **34**, 35
spag bol mac and cheese **66**, 67
traditional Bolognese **64**, 65
bread 20
  bread dumplings 98, **99**
  dump and bake bread **48**, 49
broccoli
  broccoli slice 84, **85**
  Chinese-style broccoli beef 118, **119**
browning 11, 12
butter alternatives 14
butter chicken pasta 62, **63**
butternut squash
  chickpea and butternut squash dahl 78, **79**
  creamy butternut squash pasta **70**, 71

C

Cajun pork and mash **86**, 87
cake, banana peach **142**, 143
cannellini bean, Spanish chicken and sweetcorn stew 38, **39**
carrot
  comforting chicken soup with bread dumplings 98, **99**
  hearty goulash soup **28**, 29
  lamb tagine 128, **129**
  proper beef stew and dumplings **34**, 35
  smoky pork and bean stew 42, **43**
  traditional Bolognese **64**, 65
celery
  comforting chicken soup with bread dumplings 98, **99**
  hidden veg tomato soup 30, **31**
  proper beef stew and dumplings **34**, 35
  traditional Bolognese **64**, 65
Cheddar cheese
  broccoli slice 84, **85**
  courgette and tomato risotto 90, **91**
  creamy butternut squash pasta **70**, 71

dump and bake bread **48**, 49
dumplings **34**, 35
hodgepodge shortcut lasagne 68, **69**
meatballs in tomato sauce 56–7, **58–9**
mushroom risotto 94, **95**
ricotta and tuna stuffed giant pasta shells 72, **73**
spag bol mac and cheese **66**, 67
cheese
  to avoid 17
  hodgepodge shortcut lasagne 68, **69**
  jacket potatoes with cheesy chilli 132–3, **134–5**
  meatballs in tomato sauce 56–7, **58–9**
  ricotta and tuna stuffed giant pasta shells 72, **73**
  spag bol mac and cheese **66**, 67
  see also Cheddar cheese; cream cheese
cheese alternatives 14, 16
chia egg 15
chicken
  butter chicken pasta 62, **63**
  chicken Kyiv pasta **60**, 61
  jacket potatoes with cheesy chilli 132–3, **134–5**
  comforting chicken soup with bread dumplings 98, **99**
  easy chicken and mushroom shawarma **120**, 121
  garlic teriyaki chicken noodles 114, **115**
  Nina's favourite tender lemon garlic chicken **92**, 93
  peanut butter chicken curry **100**, 101
  pulled chicken tikka **130**, 131
  Spanish chicken and sweetcorn stew 38, **39**
  turkey chilli **80**, 81
  Turkish chicken stew **44**, 45
chickpea
  chickpea and butternut squash dahl 78, **79**
  lamb tagine 128, **129**
  sweet potato and chickpea curry **96**, 97
chilli (dish), turkey **80**, 81
Chinese-style mushroom curry **116**, 117
Chinese-style broccoli beef 118, **119**
Chinese-style spare ribs 108, **109**
chorizo, freezer raid veg stew **40**, 41
coconut milk
  chickpea and butternut squash dahl 78, **79**
  Chinese-style mushroom curry **116**, 117
  coconut potato curry 88, **89**
  peanut butter chicken curry **100**, 101
  sweet potato and chickpea curry **96**, 97
  tomato and spinach fish stew 36, **37**
  tropical rice pudding 140, **141**
conversions 151
cooking techniques 12
cooling food 18
courgette
  beef korma **106**, 107
  chicken Kyiv pasta **60**, 61
  courgette and tomato risotto 90, **91**
  meatballs in tomato sauce 56–7, **58–9**
  Turkish chicken stew **44**, 45
cream 9
  beef korma **106**, 107
  lamb curry 112, **113**
  pulled chicken tikka **130**, 131
  see also soured cream

cream alternatives 14
cream cheese
  broccoli slice 84, **85**
  chicken Kyiv pasta **60**, 61
  courgette and tomato risotto 90, **91**
  creamy butternut squash pasta **70**, 71
  leek and potato soup 26, **27**
  spag bol mac and cheese **66**, 67
cream cheese alternatives 14
crème fraîche, leek and potato soup 26, **27**
crumble, fruity 144, **145**
curries
  beef korma **106**, 107
  chickpea and butternut squash dahl 78, **79**
  Chinese-style mushroom curry **116**, 117
  coconut potato curry 88, **89**
  lamb curry 112, **113**
  peanut butter chicken curry **100**, 101
  pulled chicken tikka **130**, 131
  sweet potato and chickpea curry **96**, 97

D

dahl, chickpea and butternut squash 78, **79**
dairy-free cooking 14
defrosting food 19
deglazing 12
dietary requirements 17
dip, garlic **120**, 121
dumplings

bread dumplings 98, **99**
proper beef stew and dumplings 34, 35

E

egg wash alternatives 15
egg-free cooking 15
egg(s)
  banana peach cake **142**, 143
  bread dumplings 98, **99**
  raw 17
entertaining kids 21
equipment 10–11
evaporated milk, banana peach cake **142**, 143

F

fakeaways 103–21
fats, saturated 17
fish
  ricotta and tuna stuffed giant pasta shells 72, **73**
  tomato and spinach fish stew 36, **37**
flax egg 15
food waste 20
foods to avoid 17
freezer raid veg stew **40**, 41
freezing/frozen food 9, 18–19, 20
fridges 18, 20
fruit
  fruit bowls 20
  fruity crumble 144, **145**
  see also specific fruit

G

gammon in a mustard glaze 136, **137**
garlic
  garlic dip **120**, 121
  garlic teriyaki chicken noodles 114, **115**
  Nina's favourite tender lemon garlic chicken **92**, 93
glaze, mustard 136, **137**
gluten-free cooking 15
goulash, hearty goulash soup **28**, 29
gravy, chicken 132–3, **134–5**
Greek yogurt
  butter chicken pasta 62, **63**
  dump and bake bread **48**, 49
  garlic dip **120**, 121
  lamb curry 112, **113**
  pulled chicken tikka **130**, 131
green bean, freezer raid veg stew **40**, 41

H

haricot bean
  freezer raid veg stew **40**, 41
  jacket potatoes with cheesy chilli 132–3, **134–5**
  Spanish chicken and sweetcorn stew 38, **39**
herbs 9, 11, 20
honey 17

I

ingredients 10–11
  see also specific ingredients

K

kidney bean
   jacket potatoes with cheesy chilli 132–3, **134–5**
   Mexican soup **32**, 33
   turkey chilli **80**, 81
knives 10
korma, beef **106**, 107

L

lamb
   hearty goulash soup **28**, 29
   lamb curry 112, **113**
   lamb tagine 128, **129**
lasagne, hodgepodge shortcut 68, **69**
leek
   hidden veg tomato soup 30, **31**
   leek and potato soup 26, **27**
lemon
   Nina's favourite tender lemon garlic chicken **92**, 93
lentil(s) (red), chickpea and butternut squash dahl 78, **79**

M

mac and cheese, spag bol **66**, 67
mascarpone cheese, hodgepodge shortcut lasagne 68, **69**
mash **86**, 87
meat replacements 15–16
meatballs in tomato sauce 56–7, **58–9**

Mexican soup **32**, 33
milk 9
   chicken Kyiv pasta **60**, 61
   creamy butternut squash pasta **70**, 71
   dump and bake bread **48**, 49
   hodgepodge shortcut lasagne 68, **69**
   leek and potato soup 26, **27**
   tropical rice pudding 140, **141**
   see also evaporated milk
milk alternatives 14
mushroom
   Chinese-style mushroom curry **116**, 117
   easy chicken and mushroom shawarma **120**, 121
   garlic teriyaki chicken noodles 114, **115**
   mushroom ragù 82, **83**
   mushroom risotto 94, **95**
   see also porcini mushroom (dried)
mustard glaze 136, **137**

N

noodles, garlic teriyaki chicken 114, **115**
nut-free cooking 16
nut(s) 17

O

oat(s), fruity crumble 144, **145**
orzotto, pork and apple 54, **55**

P

Parmesan cheese, meatballs in tomato sauce 56–7, **58–9**
passata
   freezer raid veg stew **40**, 41
   hodgepodge shortcut lasagne 68, **69**
   lamb curry 112, **113**
   meatballs in tomato sauce 56–7, **58–9**
   mushroom ragù 82, **83**
   ricotta and tuna stuffed giant pasta shells 72, **73**
   spag bol mac and cheese **66**, 67
   Spanish chicken and sweetcorn stew 38, **39**
   tomato and spinach fish stew 36, **37**
   traditional Bolognese **64**, 65
pasta 51–73
   butter chicken pasta 62, **63**
   chicken Kyiv pasta **60**, 61
   creamy butternut squash pasta **70**, 71
   hodgepodge shortcut lasagne 68, **69**
   meatballs in tomato sauce 56–7, **58–9**
   pork and apple orzotto 54, **55**
   ricotta and tuna stuffed giant pasta shells 72, **73**
   spag bol mac and cheese **66**, 67
   traditional Bolognese **64**, 65

peach
  banana peach cake **142**, 143
  fruity crumble 144, **145**
  tropical rice pudding 140, **141**
peanut butter chicken curry **100**, 101
pear, winter-spiced poached plums and pears **146**, 147
pea(s)
  Chinese-style mushroom curry **116**, 117
  freezer raid veg stew **40**, 41
  ricotta and tuna stuffed giant pasta shells 72, **73**
pepper
  hearty goulash soup **28**, 29
  hidden veg tomato soup 30, **31**
  sweet and sour pork **110**, 111
pineapple
  sweet and sour pork **110**, 111
  tropical rice pudding 140, **141**
plum
  fruity crumble 144, **145**
  winter-spiced poached plums and pears **146**, 147
porcini mushroom (dried)
  easy aubergine stew 46, **47**
  mushroom ragù 82, **83**
  mushroom risotto 94, **95**
porcini mushroom powder (dried)
  mushroom ragù 82, **83**
  spag bol mac and cheese **66**, 67
pork
  Cajun pork and mash **86**, 87
  Chinese-style spare ribs 108, **109**
  pork and apple orzotto 54, **55**
  pulled pork **126**, 127
  smoky pork and bean stew 42, **43**
  spag bol **66**, 67
  Sunday dinner pork belly **138**, 139
  sweet and sour pork **110**, 111
  see also gammon
porridge oat(s), fruity crumble 144, **145**
potato
  Cajun pork and mash **86**, 87
  coconut potato curry 88, **89**
  hearty goulash soup **28**, 29
  jacket potatoes with cheesy chilli 132–3, **134–5**
  leek and potato soup 26, **27**
  Nina's favourite tender lemon garlic chicken **92**, 93
  proper beef stew and dumplings **34**, 35
  Turkish chicken stew **44**, 45

R

ragù, mushroom 82, **83**
raisin(s), lamb tagine 128, **129**
reducing 12
reheating foods 19
rice
  courgette and tomato risotto 90, **91**
  mushroom risotto 94, **95**
  tropical rice pudding 140, **141**
rice drinks 17
ricotta cheese
  hodgepodge shortcut lasagne 68, **69**
  ricotta and tuna stuffed giant pasta shells 72, **73**
risotto
  courgette and tomato 90, **91**
  mushroom 94, **95**
roux 12

S

salt 11, 16
sauce, tomato 56–7, **58–9**
sautéing 12
shawarma, easy chicken and mushroom **120**, 121
shellfish 14, 17
slow cookers
  choosing the right shape and size 8
  efficiency 9
  heat settings 9
  how to use 8–9
  recipe adaptations 9, 14–17
soups 23–49
  comforting chicken soup with bread dumplings 98, **99**
  hearty goulash **28**, 29
  hidden veg tomato soup 30, **31**
  leek and potato soup 26, **27**
  Mexican soup **32**, 33
soured cream 9
soy sauce 17

spag bol mac and cheese **66**, 67
Spanish chicken and sweetcorn stew 38, **39**
spare ribs, Chinese-style 108, **109**
spices 9
spinach
  coconut potato curry 88, **89**
  sweet potato and chickpea curry **96**, 97
  tomato and spinach fish stew 36, **37**
stews 23–49
  easy aubergine stew 46, **47**
  freezer raid veg stew **40**, 41
  proper beef stew and dumplings **34**, 35
  smoky pork and bean stew 42, **43**
  Spanish chicken and sweetcorn stew 38, **39**
  tomato and spinach fish stew 36, **37**
  Turkish chicken stew **44**, 45
storing food 18–19, 20
sugar 16, 17
sweet potato and chickpea curry **96**, 97
sweet and sour pork **110**, 111
sweetcorn
  freezer raid veg stew **40**, 41
  hidden veg tomato soup 30, **31**
  jacket potatoes with cheesy chilli 132–3, **134–5**
  Mexican soup **32**, 33
  Spanish chicken and sweetcorn stew 38, **39**
  turkey chilli **80**, 81

T

tagine, lamb 128, **129**
thickening 12
tofu 16
tomato
  chickpea and butternut squash dahl 78, **79**
  courgette and tomato risotto 90, **91**
  easy aubergine stew 46, **47**
  freezer raid veg stew **40**, 41
  hearty goulash soup **28**, 29
  hidden veg tomato soup 30, **31**
  hodgepodge shortcut lasagne 68, **69**
  lamb curry 112, **113**
  lamb tagine 128, **129**
  jacket potatoes with cheesy chilli 132–3, **134–5**
  meatballs in tomato sauce 56–7, **58–9**
  Mexican soup **32**, 33
  spag bol mac and cheese **66**, 67
  sweet potato and chickpea curry **96**, 97
  tomato and spinach fish stew 36, **37**
  traditional Bolognese **64**, 65
  turkey chilli **80**, 81
  see also passata
traditional Bolognese **64**, 65
tropical rice pudding 140, **141**
tuna and ricotta stuffed giant pasta shells 72, **73**
turkey chilli **80**, 81
Turkish chicken stew **44**, 45

V

vanilla extract 16
vegetables
  hidden veg tomato soup 30, **31**
  see also specific vegetables

W

weekend indulgence recipes 123–49
weeknight recipes, easy 75–101

Y

yogurt
  beef korma **106**, 107
  see also Greek yogurt
yogurt alternatives 14

Thank you's

A big thank you to Lucy Upton for dietetic consultancy, Kathy Steer and Hello Daly for pulling this edition together, Lu Cottle for recipe testing, Sarah Epton for proofreading, and Lisa Footitt for the index.

About the author

Rebecca Wilson is a mum to Nina, a Sunday Times bestselling author, and founder of What Mummy Makes and her own food channel Rebecca Wilson. Her mission is to make family mealtimes easy for everyone and to show parents and carers that introducing solid foods can be fun, exciting, easy, and most importantly... delicious! She creates recipes for the whole family, so that babies reaching their weaning milestone at six months old can eat the same meal together with their older siblings – and even the adults too!

You can find Rebecca over on her Instagram channel @rebeccawilsonfood where she shares quick and easy meal ideas that are suitable for all the family to enjoy together.

To find out more head to @rebeccawilsonfood on Instagram or www.rebeccawilson.com.

FOOD NOTES

All-rounder potatoes are equivalent to all-purpose varieties in the US – Yukon Gold is a good example.

Egg sizes given in recipes are UK. US sizes are as follows:

UK medium = US large

UK large = US extra-large

DISCLAIMER

Those following strict allergen diets should always check the packet for guidance about suitability. The advice given in this book is based on the UK national health system guidance for family eating and baby weaning, therefore if you live outside of the UK and are ever in doubt, refer to your own country's guidance for new parents.

DK LONDON

Editorial Director Cara Armstrong
Project Editor Izzy Holton
Design Manager Tania Gomes
Production Editor David Almond
Production Controller Kariss Ainsworth
Art Director Maxine Pedliham
Publishing Director Stephanie Jackson

Editorial Kathy Steer
Design Hello Daly

First published in Great Britain in 2025 by
Dorling Kindersley Limited
20 Vauxhall Bridge Road,
London SW1V 2SA

The authorised representative in the EEA is
Dorling Kindersley Verlag GmbH. Arnulfstr. 124,
80636 Munich, Germany

Text copyright © 2025 Rebecca Wilson
Rebecca Wilson has asserted her right to
be identified as the author of this work.

Copyright © 2025 Dorling Kindersley Limited
A Penguin Random House Company
10 9 8 7 6 5 4 3 2 1
001–356164–Sept/2025

All rights reserved.
No part of this publication may be reproduced, stored in or introduced into a retrieval system, or transmitted, in any form, or by any means (electronic, mechanical, photocopying, recording, or otherwise), without the prior written permission of the copyright owner.
DK values and supports copyright. Thank you for respecting intellectual property laws by not reproducing, scanning or distributing any part of this publication by any means without permission. By purchasing an authorised edition, you are supporting writers and artists and enabling DK to continue to publish books that inform and inspire readers. No part of this publication may be used or reproduced in any manner for the purpose of training artificial intelligence technologies or systems. In accordance with Article 4(3) of the DSM Directive 2019/790, DK expressly reserves this work from the text and data mining exception.

A CIP catalogue record for this book
is available from the British Library.
ISBN: 978-0-2417-9043-4

Printed and bound in the United Kingdom

www.dk.com

This book was made with Forest Stewardship Council™ certified paper – one small step in DK's commitment to a sustainable future. Learn more at www.dk.com/uk/information/sustainability